FEATURES

AUTUMN 2021•NUMBER 29

T0163638

 Plough

INSIGHTS

ARTS & LETTERS

DEPARTMENTS

WEB EXCLUSIVES

plough.com/web29

Plough
PLOUGH.COM

EDITOR: Peter Mommsen
SENIOR EDITORS: Maureen Swinger, Sam Hine, Susannah Black
EDITOR-AT-LARGE: Caitrin Keiper
MANAGING EDITORS: Maria Hine, Dori Moody
POETRY EDITOR: A. M. Juster
DESIGNERS: Rosalind Stevenson, Miriam Burleson
CREATIVE DIRECTOR: Clare Stober
COPY EDITORS: Wilma Mommsen, Priscilla Jensen
FACT CHECKER: Suzanne Quinta
MARKETING DIRECTOR: Trevor Wiser
UK EDITION: Ian Barth
CONTRIBUTING EDITORS: Joy Clarkson, Leah Libresco Sargeant, Brandon McGinley, Jake Meador
FOUNDING EDITOR: Eberhard Arnold (1883–1935)

Plough Quarterly No. 29: Beyond Borders
Published by Plough Publishing House, ISBN 978-1-63608-044-4
Copyright © 2021 by Plough Publishing House. All rights reserved.

EDITORIAL OFFICE
151 Bowne Drive
Walden, NY 12586
T: 845.572.3455
info@plough.com

SUBSCRIBER SERVICES
PO Box 8542
Big Sandy, TX 75755
T: 800.521.8011
subscriptions@plough.com

United Kingdom
Brightling Road
Robertsbridge
TN32 5DR
T: +44(0)1580.883.344

Australia
4188 Gwydir Highway
Elsmore, NSW
2360 Australia
T: +61(0)2.6723.2213

Plough Quarterly (ISSN 2372-2584) is published quarterly by
Plough Publishing House, PO Box 398, Walden, NY 12586.
Individual subscription $32 / £24 / €28 per year.
Subscribers outside the United Kingdom and European Union pay in US dollars.
Periodicals postage paid at Walden, NY 12586 and at additional mailing offices.
POSTMASTER: Send address changes to
Plough Quarterly, PO Box 8542, Big Sandy, TX 75755.

Front cover: Agim Sulaj, *Escape*, pencil drawing on paper, 2006. Used by permission.
Inside front cover: Jarosław Koziara, *Free Flow*, land artwork, 2017. Used by permission.
Back cover: Angelina Quic Ixtamer, *Canoe Overhead*, oil on canvas, 2017. Used by permission, with thanks to Lynn Persson. More information at *terraexperience.com* and *terradollclothes.com*.

ABOUT THE COVER:
In searching for cover art for this issue, we sought to convey the importance of going beyond the barriers that arise — between countries, between religions, or even between neighbors — to connect with others, while still recognizing that such borders do exist. The image we are using, by Albanian-born artist Agim Sulaj, depicts a border but also a person who has found a creative way to go beyond. The hand reminds us that this act of reaching out is a step taken by individuals, and is not dependent on new governments, better laws, or improved social structures.

FORUM ≈
LETTERS FROM READERS

This Forum features selected responses to *Plough*'s Summer 2021 issue, "Creatures: The Nature Issue." (For a fuller conversation, see the digital version at *Plough.com/Forum28*.) The Forum is a place for commissioned responses by other writers to the questions raised by our authors, and for letters from you, our readers. Send contributions to *letters@plough.com*, with your name and town or city. Contributions may be edited for length and clarity, and may be published in any medium.

DOG EYEBROWS AND CREATION

On Peter Mommsen's "The Book of the Creatures": Thanks to Peter Mommsen for his essay on reading the book of nature, and his dog's expressive eyebrows. John Cheever wrote that he woke every single morning to the realization of how much he loved his dog. My own dogs smile for the camera, tilting their heads to demonstrate they're paying attention.

Less accessible expressions of nature are also godly. My daughter was recently given a just-hatched Australian crested gecko, only slightly bigger than her thumb. With peach-colored, silk-soft skin, Chickpea slurps up banana smoothie, and sips water from a tiny plastic cup. Christina built her a vivarium, filling the tank with earth aerated by microscopic insects that arrived by UPS. She added Hudson River driftwood and green plants. For hours, Chickpea rests on a leaf, breathing in and out. She has no appointments, no deadlines. Smooth and cool to the touch, she just is. From her, Christina says she's learning an alternate way of being.

Mommsen bestows high-octane attention, with reference to many sound texts, on the book of nature: "All this strikes one powerfully as so obviously good," he writes, "that it seems to suggest a Goodness behind it all." Awesome.

Peggy Ellsberg,
Ossining, New York

CONVERSION THROUGH BEAUTY

On Ian Marcus Corbin's "The Abyss of Beauty": Corbin's description of his near-epiphany on seeing his urban "weed-tree" in a totally different light as it becomes "something marvelous" is beautiful. Perhaps we can indeed "see ourselves to life."

Paul wrote that "since the creation of the world God's invisible qualities – namely his eternal power and divine nature – have been clearly seen, being understood from what has been made." Brother Lawrence's epiphany, in *The Practice of the Presence of God*, on realizing that the leafless tree before him would become something quite other as its "dead" branches blossomed and bore fruit likewise led him to recognize his Creator's hand, blessing his whole life, and those of many others.

Joanna Ray,
Corhampton, England

As a boy who grew up in a city of concrete and rats, I loved visiting my aunt, confined to a tuberculosis sanatorium. My sister and I would lie on the grass naming the animals formed by the clouds passing by, a luxury we didn't have at home. We made friends with the children of other patients, and played games. One was looking for lost coins in the grass where people picnicked with their hospitalized relatives. One day we found about three dollars' worth and shared the bounty between us. We all ran to the Good Humor truck. Fond memories.

I am now close to eighty. I'd love to lie in the grass, but it would take a troop of Marines to get me vertical. So, I go into my yard, where my wife has made a sanctuary for birds, rabbits, and the occasional groundhog. In this primeval forest, I sit and meditate, pray, and write. I find peace in the wilds of my yard, and I find God. I wrestle with myself, but God lifts me from the depths of my depression and my worries. I think of God who thinks of me. I live in the comfort of the Sabbath, God's day of rest in the grace of our world. I am in the peace of my wildness.

Russell Kendall Carter
Fredericksburg, Virginia

Can beauty be "true"? This is one of the questions that Corbin's poignant essay invites us to explore, especially in the relation beauty bears to suffering. Can we trust the sense beauty gestures to of what Vaclav Havel called "ultimate happiness and harmony," one that seems somehow to exist beyond the brutality of a fallen world?

Corbin suggests "we can't finally know, of course," and while I sympathize with his sense of ambiguity, I believe that we can indeed "know" that beauty is truer than evil because it arrives not just as an experience, but as a narrative. Beauty is intimately connected with suffering because it comes to renew what pain and destruction have stolen; the vision of a healed cosmos, the undoing of brutality, a world, not broken, but radically renewed.

Beauty allows us to "taste and see" the hope of a joy that endures beyond the touch of death, one that could even bring us back to life. Because of this, there is an empowering aspect to beauty. Only at the end of the essay does Corbin begin to describe what I believe is an integral element to beauty: it challenges us to act.

Beauty can restore, not just our vision, but our identity, the sense of ourselves as agents either of beauty or evil in this

world. This is why Corbin can describe Havel's vision of beauty in the midst of prison as "something like a conversion experience," with the evidence of his life being that he worked to embody the vision of wholeness that visited him. This is, I believe, what our encounters with beauty are always beckoning us toward: the knowledge that we may be healed, the astonishing invitation to walk in the ways of beauty and thus to become healers ourselves.

Corbin is right in his closing: it is a demanding work of attention and reception, yes, but also of action. Beauty asks us to enflesh what we have seen, to order, to create, to save, to heal. But the farther we walk in the light of its vision, the more deeply, I believe, we will know its truth.

Sarah Clarkson,
West Sussex, England

BODIES SPEAK

On Leah Libresco Sargeant's "Let the Body Testify": Christians are often pressured to follow a political agenda that would value either women's bodies or

unborn bodies. We desperately need voices like Libresco's to call us to a comprehensive ethic. Many Christians are discipled by competing political parties or cable news outlets, and someone who cares equally about misogyny and abortion is looked at sideways.

But what if we let the teaching of Christ guide us?

What if the same impulse that causes pro-life people to cry out for the lives of unborn human beings who are killed every day also caused us to address sexism, the environment, racism, classism, war, and criminal justice?

What if those who espouse liberal principles of dignity, equity, and justice allowed the same impulse to extend that compassion toward unborn human beings? "My body, my choice" makes no sense when we're speaking of the body of another being. How can we claim that a baby girl's body doesn't matter because it's housed in her mother's body? How can we use "viability" as an excuse to kill a person once we've recognized how interdependent the human family is? Is a person's life

Peer Christensen,
Crabapple Study,
oil on canvas
(detail)

Shai Yossef,
Touchdown,
oil on canvas

really worthless because the natural stage of development she's in requires her to live in her mother's body and depend upon her for sustenance? Why does this change once she's born? She continues to be absolutely dependent upon her mother for care and nourishment. Is breastmilk that different from amniotic fluid? Is the warm embrace of a mother's arms that different from the warm embrace of her womb?

I'm pro-life when it comes to abortion – and healthcare, the environment, economics, and criminal justice. Pro-life and liberal ideals only make sense together.

Can we allow our beliefs and practice to be formed by the teaching of Christ rather than our political party? Can we see the image of God in every human being? May it be so in Jesus' name.

Israel Michael Steinmetz,
San Antonio, Texas

This is spot-on about how the primacy of the individual has structured our society. How weakness, infirmity, and poverty are made invisible, by sequestering the very young, the very old, and the very poor out of our sight in nurseries, nursing homes, and ghettos. All the political battles going on right now are being fought within that framework. The disregard for care workers and educators is testimony to that structure. You can be an independent woman (or man) only for so long before illness and age catch up with you.

Jesus told us to let our light shine because the light makes invisible people visible. His encounters with the lame, the blind, the diseased, women, children, the marginalized are recorded in scripture as examples for us. We must let his light become our light, by which we rehumanize ourselves and others.

Al Owski,
Commerce Township, Michigan

LORDSHIP, NOT TYRANNY

On Pater Edmund Waldstein's "The Lords of Nature": Head transplants? Perhaps we've mistaken our model of reality for reality itself. "Mind" and "matter" are categories that help us understand ourselves but it doesn't follow that the reality of which they are a model is so tidy. Consciousness (mind) cannot be reduced to purely materialistic explanations – matter in motion. Yet mind does appear enabled by matter, and mind affects matter. There is a

unity. Mind and matter cannot be torn asunder without changing both. Much like we can't observe a particle or live in the world without changing either.

What we force apart we then clumsily try to push back together. Neither human rationalism nor Romantic authenticity (a compelling division of ourselves) are complete renderings of self. So we grasp at both to build a more complete representation of humanness – matter with mind, thinking with feeling – but fail to see the trap of subjectivism and relativism. We cannot engineer the merging of rationalism and authenticity in a purely objective way unless we have a Feserian "vantage point" outside both. And we don't. The Christianity that "understands creation as deeply rational," provides that vantage point in God. He is the Lord of creation. We are just lords.

That we think we are Lords is the scariest thing about modernity. Lords with flimsy self-constructed selves, "formed and re-formed by the arbitrary dictates of our will."

Jessica T. Miskelly,
Southern Highlands, Australia

BACK TO THE LAND, AGAIN

On John Kempf's "Regenerative Agriculture": When I read Kempf's article on regenerative agriculture, I immediately emailed it to my grandson who's just getting started in agriculture (he had a rather unfortunate experience with pigs in college and lost a bit of

Artwork by Shai Yossef. Used by permission from the artist

money). Turns out he was reading on the same topic. We had a good conversation; I recommended Wendell Berry's writings. Our abuse of the land has diminished our inheritance. Now, faced with floods in some areas and drought in others, we are being forced to adapt to save what we have left.

John Scott,
Batavia, Illinois

Decades ago, my forestry teacher advised us to ask some questions each time we observed a particular forest stand: Who are you? Where do you come from (that is, how did you develop)? Where are you going (that is, how will you develop)?

This means I have to see this forest as a specific part of God's creation, often very much influenced by clear cuts of my ancestors, perhaps degraded, growing on a specific site and soil, having a specific natural vegetation mix.

Each stand, each forest, is an individual. Investigating its history shows me a great deal. In this way I develop a relationship with it. For me such a relationship to a piece of forest land is the key to finding the right steps for any kind of tending, harvesting, promoting natural regeneration, choosing the species of trees to be planted, etc.

A personal relationship with Jesus is the key to becoming a real disciple of Christ. A personal relationship to the land which has been entrusted to me as a forester is essential in order to treat it in the best way – for me and for

future generations. I am appointed as a ruler over God's creation (Gen. 1:26–28) but every ruler who as a king does not have a relationship with and love for his people, his land, will become an exploiting tyrant and not a steward (Gen. 2:15).

Hans-Peter Lang,
Wieselburg, Austria

FROM AN INCARCERATED READER

I am a prisoner of the state of Ohio currently residing at Grafton Correctional Institution. I received a complimentary issue of *Plough* in the mail, and in a letter that accompanied it, you invited suggestions for future coverage. I've got some ideas.

Having been incarcerated for the last fourteen years, my exposure to the outside world is limited. In 2009, I came across a book in the prison library from *Plough* – Eberhard Arnold's *Inner Land*. Inside of the book was a mail-in card requesting more information. I received a response from Jeremy Wright, then of Spring Valley Bruderhof. I've carried on correspondence with Mr. Wright over the years; he's sent me books, and I've mentioned to him how my exposure to *Plough* publications proved formative for my personal spiritual growth and development.

I've been enjoying the issues of the *Plough Quarterly* that I have received and am sincerely thankful for this blessing. I want to extend my gratitude

to you and everybody at *Plough*. I know you all will be blessed abundantly for this great work for God's kingdom.

For the past decade, I've worked as an aide facilitating classes (many of them faith-based) for prisoners. The last four years I spent as a mentor working one-on-one with men as well as running classes. Many of the issues that lead people to prison have been touched on in *Plough* (e.g., poverty, addiction, violence, veterans, mental illness). Yet, I have not seen very much on incarceration itself. (There was one short article recently, I believe.) Incarceration tends to be an overlooked issue because it is seen as the result of personal choice. The reality is far more complicated than that.

I hope you won't take this letter as criticism – far from it – it's high praise. I would just like to see some of these problems, so prevalent in American society, addressed more frequently.

Ryan Salim,
Grafton, Ohio

Of the Hawk,
from the
Aberdeen
Bestiary

FAMILY&
FRIENDS
AROUND THE WORLD

Photograph courtesy of Colorado Sun

Preparing dinner at Casa de Paz, Aurora, Colorado

Casa de Paz

One small Colorado home has become a place of refuge and support for thousands of immigrants upon their release from detention centers.

Charles E. Moore

"Last night I was hungry, and I found food for myself. I was thirsty, and I found something to drink. But what about my neighbors who can't fend for themselves?" This thought inspired Sarah Jackson to start Casa de Paz, an organization that offers shelter, meals, plane or bus tickets, rides, and emotional support to immigrants released

from the US Immigration and Customs Enforcement detention center in Aurora, Colorado. Her mission? "To reunite families separated by immigrant detention, one simple act of love at a time."

Sarah founded Casa de Paz in 2012, after she traveled to the US-Mexico border. The stories she heard and the individuals she met there motivated her to do more. She started hosting recently released detainees in her tiny two-bedroom apartment across from the detention center until she raised enough money to rent a bigger house.

Tucked in a cul-de-sac fifteen minutes' drive from the detention center, Casa de Paz blends in among the many suburban homes. Visitors cross a doormat with the word "Home" emblazoned on it, the letter "o" replaced by a heart. The house is decorated with photos of travelers who have passed through. Two bedrooms on the first floor are fitted with bunk beds and closets filled with backpacks and donated supplies.

With the help of hundreds of volunteers, Casa de Paz has hosted over three thousand guests from seventy-nine countries, helping them reunite with family or find a place to go

Charles E. Moore is a writer and contributing editor to Plough. *He is a member of the Bruderhof, an intentional community movement based on Jesus' Sermon on the Mount.*

next. Sarah's book, *The House that Love Built* (Zondervan), tells the story in full.

When Covid put a stop to in-person visits at the detention center, volunteers decided to write letters. The Casa de Paz Pen Pal program now has people writing to detainees in over thirty detention centers across the country.

When people are released from the detention center, Casa on Wheels is waiting for them directly outside. The van is stocked with food, drinks, and other necessities. Volunteers start making plans to get them safely to their final destinations.

Despite the pandemic, Casa de Paz was able to raise enough money last year to purchase a larger home across from the detention center. This will now be the hub for all they do, including overseeing *las casitas*, "little homes," throughout the city. "The needs of displaced immigrants are only growing," Sarah observes. "A much wider network of welcome is needed."

It is love that drives Sarah and the volunteers. "Detention is sterile. It is unwelcoming. It is cold. It is a prison. Casa de Paz is the complete opposite. Guests can feel like they are at home, even if just for a short while. Many guests have walked into our home, stopped, and looked around and said something to the effect of, 'I feel the love that is in this place.' I love that. It's what keeps all of us going."

Find out more about Casa de Paz at *casa-depazcolorado.org*, and about "Welcome Strangers," the award-winning twenty-minute documentary short about Casa de Paz at *welcomestrangersfilm.com*.

The Pilsdon Community

On the Dorset coast, a farm offers community, work, and sanctuary to those who need healing and a new direction.

Tobias Jones

The Pilsdon Community was founded in 1958 by a visionary Anglican priest, Percy Smith, and his wife, Gaynor, who had both been inspired by the story of Nicholas Ferrar's seventeenth-century religious community at Little Gidding. Most people first glimpse the community from the Iron Age hill fort, Pilsdon Pen, which overlooks the green fields of the Marshwood Vale and, just beyond, the Dorset coastline. There, far below, is the three-story manor house with its grassy quadrangle created by barns, stables, looseboxes, pigsties, and other outbuildings. Its twelve acres have all the usual greenhouses, vegetable patches, and livestock you would expect of an intentional community, plus a medieval stone church by the stream.

It's a community whose founding purpose is to offer sanctuary to people in a period of crisis in their lives. There are usually about half a dozen community members and twenty or so guests, some of whom have lived there for many years. There are also weekend visitors and volunteers. There's a regular rhythm to the community, with bells announcing meals and prayers, which are usually drawn from the Society of St Francis's daily office, *Celebrating Common Prayer*.

Garden meeting at Pilsdon community, March 2021

Tobias Jones is the cofounder of Windsor Hill Wood, and the author of Utopian Dreams *and* A Place of Refuge.

Eyvind Earle,
Pine Branch,
gouache, 1955
(detail)

Percy Smith called Pilsdon "a school for sinners, not a museum of saints," and it's a working farm which often feels distinguished by its humility and simplicity. There's a lot of mud and manure and earthy humor. Pilsdon doesn't do branding, or franchising, or even shout about itself to the world. But it's a place where agricultural parables suddenly seem to make sense, and where broken people are given the time, and love, to make sense of themselves and their wounds. While there's not a formal, therapeutic program, the combination of a drink- and drug-free space with lots of good food, companionship, manual labor, and mentoring often helps people begin to put their lives back together.

Pilsdon is gradually opening up to new people as Covid restrictions ease. Please visit *pilsdon.org.uk* for more information.

Winners of the First Annual Rhina Espaillat Poetry Award

On August 24, 2021, *Plough* announced the winners of the first Rhina Espaillat Poetry Award in a livestreamed event with Rhina P. Espaillat and *Plough* poetry editor A. M. Juster. The award is for a poem of not more than fifty lines that reflects Espaillat's lyricism, empathy, and ability to find grace in everyday events of life.

Congratulations to winner Mhairi Owens for her poem "For the Celts," and finalists Susan de Sola for "The Hunger Winter" and Forester McClatchey for "Wreathmaking," all published in the pages of this issue.

Plough's 2021 competition attracted over five hundred poems. The 2022 competition is now open. The overall winner receives $2000. In addition, two finalists receive $250. All three will be published in *Plough*. Submit your new poems at *plough.com/poetryaward*.

Mhairi Owens is a community worker living in Fife, Scotland, who writes poetry in both English and Scots. Her work has appeared in various anthologies and journals, including *Poetry Salzburg Review, The Moth, The North,* and *The Rialto*. Her Scots poem "Shiftin" won the 2019 international Wigtown Poetry Prize.

Mhairi wrote her winning poem, "For the Celts," in response to the Hart Island Project. She is donating her prize money directly to its continued efforts to name and tell the stories of those buried in the unmarked graves of Hart Island, New York's potter's field. See the poem on page 85.

Susan de Sola is a winner of the Frost Farm Prize and the David Reid Poetry Translation Prize. Her poems have appeared in many publications, such as the *Hudson Review* and *PN Review*. Her collection, *Frozen Charlotte*, was published recently by Able Muse Press. She holds a PhD in English from Johns Hopkins University and has been a faculty member at the West Chester Poetry Conference. A native New Yorker, she lives near Amsterdam with

her family. See her poem "The Hunger Winter" on page 37.

Forester McClatchey is a poet and critic from Atlanta, Georgia. He teaches at Atlanta Classical Academy, and his poetry appears in *Oxford Poetry*, the *Hopkins Review, Pleiades, Slice,* and *Birmingham Poetry Review*, among other journals. He won the 2019 Gulf Stream Summer Poetry Competition and was a 2017 finalist in the American Literary Review poetry competition. See his poem "Wreathmaking" on page 59. ➴

© 2021 Eyvind Earle Publishing. Used by permission.

PETER MOMMSEN

On Not Knowing Esperanto

Can we move beyond borders without losing our identity?

I N 1870, the ophthalmologist L. L. Zamenhof came upon the idea with which he would make his mark in history. That year, the Russian authorities banned speaking Polish in public in his hometown of Białystok, which was then controlled by the Russian Empire though historically belonging to Poland (as it does again today). Zamenhof, as a Polish-speaking Jew in a city where tensions between Poles,

Jews, Russians, and Germans ran high, came to believe that language differences were to blame for the mutual hatreds dividing his neighbors. What if, he suggested, there were a universal second language in which people of all nationalities could speak with one another as equals? "Were there but an international language," he reasoned, "all nations would be united in a common brotherhood." So he invented

Matthew Cusick, *Firebird*, maps, enamel, plaster, and coffee grains on OSB, 2002

Esperanto, the world's most successful spoken artificial language, now searchable on Wikipedia and learnable on Duolingo.

As successes go, Esperanto's has only gone so far, attracting a mixed fan base. Enthusiastically promoted by anti-nationalist anarchists in the 1920s, its use has more recently been endorsed for Islamic study by the Ayatollah Khomeini. Today, despite an endorsement from J. R. R. Tolkien – "Back Esperanto loyally," he admonished – only a few tens of thousands speak Esperanto well; perhaps two million speak it at all. A 2005 campaign to make it the working language of the European Union sputtered. This magazine, for what it's worth, stopped publishing its Esperanto edition in the 1950s.

Is our yearning for roots doomed to lead to a heartless politics of exclusion?

Instead of Esperanto, we moderns have International Business English – the language you can hear in upscale urban areas from Bogotá to Bratislava. While IBE has become the lingua franca for people around the globe, its resemblance to Zamenhof's idealistic project ends there. IBE is first and foremost for members of the professional-managerial class. The goal of their communications is not to build a common brotherhood, but to ease the efficient functioning of borderless capitalism.

Some years back, my wife and I were visiting the Tyrol, where my family has ties. Nowadays it's an "economically vibrant" region, where as a traveler it's easy to remain ensconced in an IBE-speaking bubble of sleek hotels staffed by pleasant young hipsters from everywhere-and-nowhere in the European Union, the kind of place with a breakfast buffet piled high with the non-local fruits of globalization: Turkish melons, Moroccan figs, Honduran pitahayas.

But there's still a Tyrol that lies beyond that. We were eating pizza outdoors in the high-alpine village where my grandfather was born before World War I, when it was still part of Austria (today it belongs to Italy). Near

our table, children were playing, speaking in a local Upper German dialect that I couldn't follow. But my wife could, although this was her first time in Europe and she grew up in South Dakota. Four hundred and seventy years before, her forebears had fled from near here, as Anabaptist refugees from the vicious religious persecutions of the Reformation era; the language the children were speaking in their play was her own mother tongue, or close to it. She had roots here in a place she never knew – a sense of connectedness to a homeland, to the story of a people, that she will pass on to our own children.

Over the past decade, the yearning for this kind of rootedness, for being part of the story of a people that is bigger than oneself, has flared up as a cultural force to be reckoned with. It's the theme, for example, of Michael Brendan Dougherty's heartfelt book *My Father Left Me Ireland* (2019), in which the American-raised son of an absent Irish father tells of his quest to connect with his Irish language and homeland. In a policy-oriented vein, it is the impulse behind Yoram Hazony's *The Virtue of Nationalism* (2018), which argues that democratic governance and social solidarity is only possible when nations are also states, possessing a sovereignty that can push back against the overweening dominance of the global over-class that rigs economic and legal systems to serve its own interests.

Nor is this renewed emphasis on identity and peoplehood limited to conservatives. Ta-Nehisi Coates's *Between the World and Me* (2015), with its eloquent indictment of White supremacy in America, is at the same time a father's appeal to his son to remember who he is and who he came from: "And still I urge you to struggle. Struggle for the memory of your ancestors. Struggle for wisdom. . . . Struggle for your grandmother and grandfather, for your name." In these words is the same call to the duty of collective memory that gave power to the liberationist visions of Cuba's José Martí, of India's Gandhi, and of early Zionism's Theodor Herzl.

Counterintuitively, when you immerse yourself in your own people's story you may also become better equipped to find solidarity with other people's stories. This was impressed on me when, around 2001, I entered a prison visiting room to meet with Russell "Maroon" Shoatz, a former Black Panther whose son was my coworker at the time. Russell was then six years into what would become an unimaginable twenty-two-year stint in solitary confinement in Pennsylvania. (His story, told by Ashley Lucas, is on page 60.) He struck me as one of the most alive and self-disciplined people I'd ever met – not least thanks to the push-up-heavy workout he did for an hour daily in his cell.

Apart from exercise, I asked him, how did he manage to stay sane? Russell answered by launching into an extended riff about his voracious study of liberation movements around the world, past and present – from American Indian, Irish, and Basque to Native Hawaiian, Korean, and Aboriginal Australian. His adopted name "Maroon" referred to the maroon communities of people who had escaped from slavery, and so he was especially fascinated by different kinds of communal settlements, quizzing me about the history of my own community, the Bruderhof. Though caged in an isolation cell twenty-three hours a day, his rootedness in the story of Black liberation opened up for him a point of connection with people around the globe.

That's why I believe there's much to affirm in the desire to belong to a people and its story. By way of illustration: For me as a European-descended hybrid born with two nationalities, American and German, it's clear that part of my task as a father is to pass on to my children a consciousness of their heritage. That means pride in all that is noble and admirable in the stories of the two nations to which they belong. And it means repentance for the historic sins of their ancestors, with willing acceptance of the obligation – precisely out of honor toward these ancestors – to live lives that make sense as works of atonement. For my children, learning

how the particular nations to which they belong have ample share in both the depravities and glories of humankind's history is simply part of learning who they are.

THE DESIRE TO PRESERVE NATIONAL identity, of course, can lead to darker places, as it has when the US border service allows Central American children to die in detention facilities, or when European nations allow African families to drown in the Mediterranean. At least since 2015, when Germany and other countries admitted more than a million migrants before quickly regretting the deed, identitarian politics around the world has typically meant a lust for hard borders and for over-simple stories. The new nationalists, who in post-Christian countries love to appeal to the memory of a Christian West, applaud when governments threaten lethal force to keep out people who may be fleeing for their lives. As I write this in mid-August 2021, leaders of wealthy nations are already washing their hands of the foreseeable deaths of thousands of Afghans and Haitians to whom they seem unwilling to offer entry.

For Christians, at any rate, to support such actions is to deny the faith. It's often said that one can't quote proof texts from the Bible to mandate or forbid a government policy, and usually this holds true. There are exceptions, though, and here is one of the big ones. Throughout the Old and New Testaments rings a repeated command to care for widows and orphans and to welcome the stranger: "The alien who resides with you shall be to you as the citizen among you; you shall love the alien as yourself" (Lev. 19:34). The prophets don't present this as just a question of personal morality; the whole nation is accountable to God for its treatment of these vulnerable ones. The Book of Deuteronomy mandates a triennial tithe to provide for their support, and warns: "Cursed be anyone who deprives the alien, the orphan, and the widow of justice" (27:19). Jesus is even more emphatic: "You that are accursed,

Matthew Cusick,
Bird of Prey,
maps and
archival tape,
2007

depart from me into the eternal fire prepared for the devil and his angels; for I was hungry and you gave me no food, I was thirsty and you gave me nothing to drink, I was a stranger and you did not welcome me" (Matt. 25:41–43).

The least that we Christians in wealthy nations can do is to clamor for accepting as many persecuted migrants as our societies can accommodate. Which, if our priorities are where they should be and we fear God, is a lot.

S OUR YEARNING FOR ROOTS doomed to lead to a heartless politics of exclusion? That's only inevitable if we wed our innate desire for belonging to the coercive apparatus of the territorial state, which guards its borders with the threat of lethal violence. But why assume that national identity needs to be defended by state power and force of arms? That was a question that occupied Gustav Landauer (1870–1919), a Jewish German anarchist, socialist, and pacifist whose thought inspired the founders of the Bruderhof communities and the first kibbutz settlements in Israel.

Landauer, who tirelessly sought to promote international solidarity among workers' movements until World War I destroyed his labors, made a sharp distinction between state and national identity: "The state and its borders are lamentable chance products of the most miserable phenomena of history. Nationality, ethnicity, hereditary characteristics are

individual qualities with wonderfully deep roots that connect people to one another."

"Do Not Learn Esperanto!" is the title of one of Landauer's broadsides from 1907, directed to fellow radicals who wished to submerge national differences in a culturally deracinated *Internationale.* For Landauer, this was a false path. National identity, as he wrote earlier that same year, is a natural good, which is not bound to, still less created by, the state and its artificial borders: "Nationality is genuineness and the bond of love and spirit. It suffices on its own, and needs no state in order to live within people and to create from within them a work of beauty." He dreamed of a voluntary community of working people in which all are not only cared for, enjoying the good things of life, but what's more, are able to flourish within a rich shared culture:

> The French nation is a community of language, and thus also a spiritual association and a religious body: Rabelais, Molière, Voltaire are its princes and kings. The same goes for the German nation: the German folk song is the Magna Carta of this glorious confederation, and Goethe is king within it. So too the Jews have their unity and their Isaiah and Jesus and Spinoza.

Accordingly, Landauer deplored artificial schemes for universal brotherhood. For him, cultural commonalities and differences go to the heart of what makes a community human:

> Anarchists need to understand that the basis of both individual life and human coexistence is something that cannot be invented artificially. It is something that has to grow organically. Society as a voluntary union of humanity, for example, has grown organically. Nowadays, this union has been overgrown by a dreadful artificial product, the state. . . .
>
> Ineradicable, real difference does not only exist between peoples, it exists between all human beings. Each human being talks, thinks, and feels differently than others. In

fact, humans can understand and talk to one another because they are different. If they were all the same, they would hate one another. Total sameness is not only impossible; it would also be dreadful. . . .

Here is my advice: practice thinking and feeling as it needs to be practiced! Practice the intricacies and complexities of languages that have grown organically – especially your own! Never give up the study of your own language! And do not learn Esperanto!

Landauer believed in a voluntary socialism of deeds, and consistently strove to put his convictions into practice. Yet he never saw his vision of a community of free workers become reality. Persecuted by the German authorities for his opposition to World War I, he was murdered during the German Revolution by rightwing paramilitaries shouting anti-Semitic slurs. Up until his death, he remained a professed atheist. All the same, he seems to have intuited that the true ground for the community he sought might lie deeper even than shared nationality or language:

Once upon a time, there existed a community of the spirit that was not subject to language, much less did it stop at the borders of the state. This community was Christendom with its Dante and its Gothic architecture, which stretched from Moscow to Sicily and Spain. Its origin was like the origin of all spirit: from the heads, yearnings, and hearts of a few, and from the dully sensed sufferings and desires of the peoples. But its meaning, when once it had attained its height, was: expression, sign, and transfiguration, indeed the art, of being a community of cult and culture. Christendom with its Gothic spires and towers, with its symmetry of the asymmetrical, with its freedom in beautiful and strict togetherness, with its guilds and fraternities, was a nation in the highest and most powerful sense: the most profound penetration of economic and cultural community by the bond of the spirit.

Historians may dispute Landauer's idealized portrait of the Middle Ages. But whether or not it corresponds to the realities of medieval Europe, his "once upon a time" myth stirringly sketches out the vision that Landauer lived and died for. It's a vision that owes much to his beloved Isaiah, the prophet of peace, who spoke of the day when "all the nations shall stream" together to the eschatological Jerusalem. "They shall beat their swords into plowshares, and their spears into pruning hooks; nation shall not lift up sword against nation, neither shall they learn war any more" (Isa. 2:2–4).

Landauer's vision of Christendom, too, reflects a truth recognized by the early Christians when they interpreted Isaiah's words as foretelling the birth of the church at Pentecost. On that day, as described in the Book of Acts, people of many nationalities could communicate across language barriers yet still in their native tongues. They were of one heart and soul, and joined together to share all things in common so that all were cared for, in a voluntary community not dependent on the state. Such a community is not so distant from what Landauer, atheist though he was, longed to see.

Nor is it distant, really, from the "common brotherhood" of "all nations" for whose sake L. L. Zamenhof invented Esperanto. But it is not quite the same. In the biblical vision of humankind's ultimate future, of which the Pentecost church understood itself to be a foretaste, the New Jerusalem is a place where distinction remains – and is glorified. "By its light," writes John on Patmos, "will the nations walk, and the kings of the earth will bring their glory into it. . . . They will bring into it the glory and the honor of the nations." These nations will not have lost their languages, identities, and stories as the price of unity. They will have come, beyond borders but still as themselves, to Zion. ⤳

Quotes from Gustav Landauer are taken from "Lernt nicht Esperanto!" (1907, trans. Gabriel Kuhn) and "Dreißig sozialistische Thesen" (1907, trans. the author).

Three Kants

and a Thousand Skulls

In Rwanda, the tales
of a young student, an
Enlightenment philosopher,
and a skull-hunting colonialist
intertwine.

SIMEON WIEHLER

DEUTSCH - OSTAFRIKA

1 : 15 000 000

Opening spread: Immanuel Kant (1724–1804); Richard Kandt (1867–1918); and an unidentified University of Rwanda student contemporary with Nkurikiyumukiza Kant, for whom no photograph could be found.

SOME TWO YEARS AGO, after I gave a lecture on "building better societies," I was followed back to my office by a student with the formidable name of Nkurikiyumukiza Kant. (In the Rwandan naming system both are first names, one being African and the other Christian, French, or something noteworthy – I know several Clintons, a Reagan, and many, many young Obamas.) Kant wished to discuss further an idea he had voiced in lecture: that Rwandans had treated each other with such cruelty during the genocide because they did not love animals. While it is true that nobody here keeps pets, and that one regularly encounters rank callousness toward animals in the fields or headed for the market, it is not the sadistic, vicious cruelty that was the hallmark of Rwanda's 1994 genocide, but something closer to expedient insensitiveness, or an insufficiency of identification with the potential for suffering in other creatures.

I had skirted his proposition in lecture and Kant lost no time in bringing his famous namesake to bear him witness. Here it is, he said, jabbing his finger into a well-worn copy of Immanuel Kant's *Lectures on Ethics*: "He who is cruel to animals becomes hard also in his dealings with men. We can judge the heart of a man by his treatment of animals."

I knew Kant had come from a government-run rural high school near the bottom of the national rankings. Like the vast majority of my students he was the first in his family to attend university. As dean of the School of Social, Political and Administrative Sciences, I also knew that he was middle-of-the-pack in his university cohort. But he did stand out. He had an earnestness about him that showed fairly quickly that he wasn't attending Rwanda's premier tertiary institution for the social life. He really wanted to engage, to understand. Perhaps because of this he asked questions fearlessly.

In my travels across the continent I have encountered many like him: smart, inquisitive, soaking up knowledge like the red volcanic loam of Rwanda soaks up the first rain after the long dry season, but with family histories overflowing with suffering, dislocation, and deprivation: genocide trauma, refugee camp survival, war, and always – like background music – grinding poverty. How many African Albert Einsteins or Toni Morrisons, Nelson Mandelas or Immanuel Kants has our world never known because they dropped out of primary school to fetch firewood or pick coffee so their families could survive? They don't disappear, of course. They live out their lives in their villages: the shopkeeper who can do complex multiplications instantaneously in his head, the farmer famous for the wedding poetry he creates and memorizes while herding his cows, the wise elder whose advice has soothed troubled marriages and ended village feuds. They know the value of education and try to send their children to school, but even those that reach their local high schools face major challenges. I have visited rural high schools that had received computers from the government but did not have electricity. In others, teachers were using computers for instruction with students carefully taking notes on which icon the teacher clicked. These rural students arrive at our university and tell me they "know" computers, but have never "used" one.

So it was that Kant arrived on campus, eager to learn and unshrinking when he had a question or wanted to raise a point. I got the impression this vexed other professors, but I enjoy classroom discussion and debate and

---

Simeon Wiehler is Dean of the School of Social, Political and Administrative Sciences at the University of Rwanda.

was usually happy when Kant interrupted me in mid-sentence. Such teachable interludes often help students grapple with complex thoughts or big ideas, but his attempt to link the genocide with how Rwandans regard animals curved in from so far in left field that I stammered and brushed it aside with a wholly unsatisfactory non-answer.

I WAS REMINDED OF KANT and his animals in the months before *coronavirus* became a household word, when I was asked to join a committee set up to advise on what to do with a thousand Rwandan skulls discovered in museum storage in Berlin. They had been collected by the German explorer, psychiatrist, and colonial governor Richard Kandt between 1901 and 1907 with the double goal of defining a "racial" difference between the Tutsi and Hutu populations of Rwanda and measuring cranial capacity to support the assertion that Europeans were smarter than Africans.

The skulls had been amassed in the governor's mansion in Kigali from looted funeral locations all over the country, and from the national execution site near the palace of the traditional ruler, the *Mukama*, who continued to hold immense cultural sway even under colonialism. Kandt himself was an efficient administrator, a ruthless man with a prodigious appetite for assembling large collections pertaining to some of his more mordacious predilections: venomous snakes, lizards, poisonous spiders, crocodile skins, lion paws. Some of his collections are today on display in the very same mansion, recently converted into a museum. But his collection of skulls did not stay in Rwanda; they were shipped off to Berlin for "scientific" scrutiny, where they were eventually forgotten in storage. They survived catastrophic bombing in World War II and were rediscovered during the planning of the recently opened Humboldt Museum in Berlin, posing awkward questions about Germany's racist and colonialist past, and presenting a diplomatic predicament for Rwandan-German relations.

Since the Rwandan genocide, the country has been struggling to deal with its much more recent legacy of horror and trauma. Mass graves or scattered bones are regularly uncovered during construction excavations or when a perpetrator decides to come clean, but no one had an inkling that any Rwandan bones were in Germany, let alone a thousand human skulls. When the message arrived from the Humboldt Museum organizers, suggesting that university professors from the social sciences should assist in the diplomatic deliberations, I was asked to join the discussions.

The Humboldt Museum in Berlin

MY PATH TO RWANDA was an unusual one in the first place: I grew up in the Bruderhof communities in Pennsylvania and England. In my late teens, with no idea what I wanted to do with my life, I took a job outside the community that led me eventually to help in a Ugandan organization assisting street children. It was 1982. One year grew to thirteen, which encompassed a civil war and two coups, some successes and many failures, friends good and false, happy moments and lonely despair. I learned what fear was, and rank injustice, that children laugh and sing and play even amid deep poverty. And I learned about death. Lots of death.

I picked up the language and slowly grew into the culture – how disorienting and different it was from the Bruderhof,

or indeed from Western culture, but how, once one looked from the inside, it was logical and made its own sense of the world and of foreigners like me. Woven through all this were the street children who became my Ugandan family. Most had suffered terribly in the war, lost their families, fled their villages, and ended up in Kampala's markets, municipal dumps, and street margins. It gave me profound joy to see many of them shape those broken and painful pieces into new lives. I worked on ways that seemed to help this process and slowly evolved ambitious national plans to solve the street-children problem in its entirety, which I pushed with all involved. A healthy society, I kept repeating, will never tolerate hundreds of children begging from motorists, stealing in the markets, and sleeping on the verandas of the city.

At the time the war ended in 1986, I assumed street-child numbers in Kampala would decrease, but over the following years they increased rapidly. This conundrum, and the inability of NGO colleagues, government demographers, and a growing circle of academics to answer it, eventually led me to study this issue at Cornell University, which offered me access to knowledge and research that in those pre-internet days was impossible to obtain in Uganda. (Cornell also gave me a scholarship.) I wanted to know what strategies other countries had adopted – New York City had a huge street-child population, as did London. What did they do to address this?

Map showing the route of Richard Kandt's expedition, 1897–1901

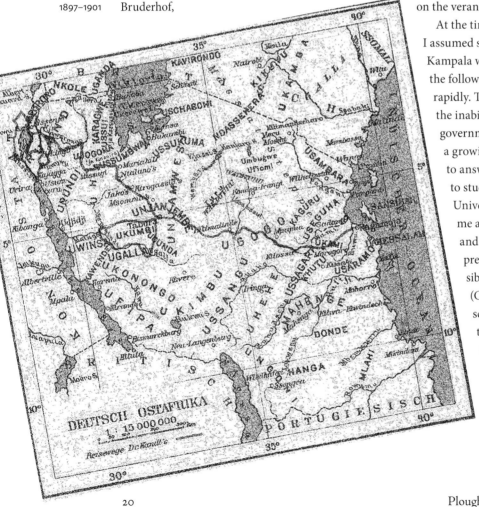

Later, doing a Fulbright-funded Africa-wide comparison of street-child programs, I met my wife-to-be in Rwanda, running a vocational training center. We were married in 2003, and when I finally finished my PhD, a teaching position opened up at the University of Rwanda – a perfect fit.

Rwanda has adopted almost the entire multipronged street-child solution I had been proposing. This included implementing universal primary education, with truancy enforcement; mandating parental responsibility for minors; banning child labor; buttressing the country's universal health insurance; setting up intervention centers; and deploying a nationwide team of social workers both to monitor the streets and to supervise family reintegration programs. All this, of course, has required long-term policy and budget commitments at the national level. But the effects have been dramatic. Today Rwanda is the only country in Africa in which you will not find children sleeping on the streets. All is not perfect, of course – no bureaucracy is – and Covid-19 has put additional stress on the system. But by and large it works. These days I teach and try to inspire Rwanda's brightest young future leaders, helping them think of better ways to solve social problems, think strategically about social change, and imagine better societies (in which there are, of course, no street children).

BUT BACK TO THOSE SKULLS. Everyone in our meetings agreed that the skulls must be brought back and respectfully interred in Rwandan soil, but engaging the nation in welcoming these remains, taken in such a different era, raises complex cultural, historical, emotional, and religious issues. How would one explain to a national audience the early-twentieth-century fascination with the pseudosciences of craniometry, phrenology, or race-intelligence hierarchies? How account for the arrogant cruelty of European colonial rule, in which a governor could amass human skulls as if they were a stamp collection?

In our meetings we discussed whether these skulls might be DNA-linked to a near relative or family, but without nationwide DNA data this is unlikely. What kind of welcoming ceremony would be appropriate? What about burial observances? When these skulls were collected, Christian missionaries had not made any converts in the country. The indigenous religion had not been entirely animist; the Great God, *Imana*, was said to spend his days traveling around the world, but at night always returned to Rwanda. But within this belief system the bones of the dead were – like clothing or the cowhide sandals everyone wore – considered the cast-off leftovers of life. The spirits of the dead were not connected to the bones but housed in tiny thatched huts behind each family dwelling; food and alcohol were offered to keep them happy (an unhappy spirit would surely cause problems). Westerners, for whom human bones hold, even in death, something of the essence of the person who once animated them, could consider this: We discard cut hair and fingernail clippings because, once cut, we perceive them as possessing no human essence. In many traditional African cultures if a strand of hair or a single nail-clipping lands in the wrong hands it can be a powerful means for wreaking havoc upon its erstwhile owner. Hair and fingernails were imbued with life-power; bones not so much.

> **Truly opposing genocide or colonialism, racism or discrimination does not start from moral superiority but through deep humility.**

Much of this age-old culture has changed. In the course of less than two generations, the god of the occupier replaced local gods. Ancient traditions and belief systems morphed into dispositions acceptable to a powerful colonial church and coercive governing elites. This trend continued in the years following independence. Rwanda today is highly Christianized; about 95 percent self-identify as Christian. And yet in the moment of national trauma, Rwandan Christians failed to stand up for love, mercy, and tolerance, or even basic humanity. During the three months of genocide in 1994, Christians of all denominations filed out of church on Sunday mornings to slaughter their neighbors. Pastors organized the mass murder of their parishioners. Priests killed fellow priests. Nuns decapitated orphans. Bishops bulldozed churches where fleeing Tutsis had sought refuge. All on the basis of a social division which had come to represent access to power, privilege, and status. The failure of Christians (except in a tiny number of isolated cases) to stand up to the Hutu-Tutsi social divide remains an indictment of a century's worth of missionary endeavor in this part of the world.

In our meetings about the skulls we explored how to frame a national discussion around colonial barbarity and genocidal brutality, both examples of humankind's predilection for hatred and immeasurable cruelty. The conversation has become an opportunity to imagine a way out of hell. Maybe Kant's "treatment of animals" does have something to say, not because animal life is to be valued as human life, but because our attitude in this regard holds a mirror to our deepest selves, shows us the truth of our moral shallowness, the gap between our ideals and our actions.

But there is something more. Governor Kandt dehumanized Africans, treating Rwandans as mere animals whose skulls could be collected. Genocide dehumanized Tutsis; the extremist radio called them "cockroaches" and screamed for these "vermin" to be exterminated. In both historical instances we confront the stripping of the sacredness from fragile humanity, humans equated to animals to be butchered or collected. But dare we peer into this abyss without also confronting the same propensity in our own hearts, the inclination towards evil, where we have marginalized, belittled, undervalued, or hurt others whose lives are equally precious in God's eyes? Truly opposing genocide or colonialism, racism or discrimination does not start from moral superiority but through deep humility that sees fallen humanity with all its failings, and recognizes that human fallenness in our own hearts as well.

Only then can we ask ourselves if we are the systemic change that this world needs. Do we embody a shared willingness to contribute to the common good to achieve what the individual alone cannot? Are we truth-seekers? Telling the deep truth about ourselves, about our comfortable myths and imagined realities can be uncomfortable, but without truth-seeking, good cannot grow and evil clings on, like mold, in the cracks. Have we looked at the world around us and imagined what might be better and then said so? Do the small acts of our daily lives help build stronger relationships, better neighborhoods? Do our actions strengthen justice and enhance what is good in our communities? Do we pursue peace and oppose hate even in the small things, knowing that small plus small plus small can get pretty big? Will each one of us be able to say, when life nears its end, that we planted our feet determinedly on the side of good, that we struggled for what was right, that we joined with similarly-minded people and together tried to build a better society?

As we attempted to come to terms with the layered meanings of those thousand skulls, a virus was spreading in Wuhan, China, which would soon close down the university, strangle the economy, confine us in our homes for weeks at a time, and postpone all our decisions to some later date. What a humbling reminder of all we do not control on this small planet of ours.

I had one more interaction with my student Kant, who tugged at my arm in the hallway one day, just before the pandemic struck. He wanted to discuss his latest quote from the other Kant (or at least attributed to him): "We are not made rich by what we possess but by what we can do without." I told him I approved the sentiment – I was thinking, "that's very Bruderhof" – and suggested he drop by some-time for a discussion. It was not to be. A few days later he was killed in a bus accident on the treacherous mountain roads near Karongi, along with twenty-six other passengers.

At such times one feels oneself encircled by death: the death of a smart and inquisitive student, a million genocide deaths, a thousand skulls in a faraway land. But face it livingly we must: we actively engage in the inch-by-inch remaking of a post-genocide nation; we encourage young students to imagine better societies. We negotiate the repatriation of stolen human remains, because we have peered into the abyss of human depravity, glimpsed the outlines of consummate evil, and determined that in our own lives and in the lives we touch, we must stand for something diametrically opposite.

In this lies the measure: that our respect for life finds reflection in our treatment of all God's creatures, not least our human brothers and sisters; that we love our neighbor as ourselves, and do not return evil for evil, but lean toward all that is good. Or, as my student Nkurikiyu-mukiza Kant wrote in last year's exam, about how he intended to be part of building a better society: "Go into the world as peacemakers. Be courageous for what is good. Do bad to nobody. Help the weak and the poor. Treat each other with respect," he wrote, with a final evocation of his namesake's "starry skies above and the moral law within." I miss him. ➺

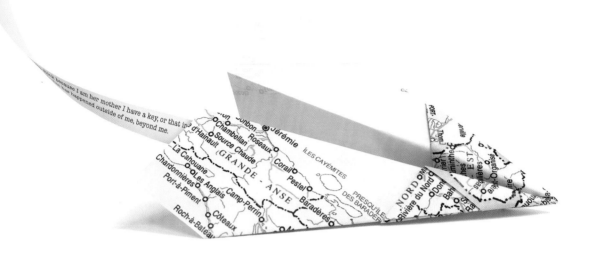

Home Is Not Just a Place

With words we build homes no separation can take away.

EDWIDGE DANTICAT

Y FIFTEEN-YEAR-OLD DAUGHTER, Mira, is taking a summer writing class online. Taught by the writer Erica Cardwell, the class is called "Writing the Self." Mira and I are both won over by the course description:

> Imagine: "The Essay" is a body of water – far-flung and teeming into the distance. And you, the writer, are alone on shore. Will you enter the water? And if so, how will you swim? Or will you stand on shore as the water splashes against your ankles?

"I wish I could take this class," I tell Mira.

What I mean is I wish I could have taken this class when I was her age. I have read most of the assigned essays. I decide to revisit some, which I read out loud to Mira. We read "When We Dead Awaken: Writing as Re-Vision" (1972) by the poet Adrienne Rich. I have been looking for something more concrete than my own enthusiasm to convince Mira that this class is an incredible gift, especially in the midst of a global pandemic and racial justice protests, at a time when we are all, writers and non-writers alike, searching for the right words

Edwidge Danticat is the author of many books, including, most recently, Everything Inside: Stories *(Knopf Publishing, 2019).*

Origami by Miriam Burleson

to describe our unique personal state, as well as the overall human condition. Then I come across Adrienne Rich's description: "Writing is re-naming."

We then read Audre Lorde's "Poetry Is Not a Luxury" (1977), where Lorde reminds us, "There are no new pains. We have felt them all already."

In an August 1979 exchange between the two women, Lorde cites her choral poem about the frequent silence around the lives and deaths of murdered Black women and girls:

"Need: A Chorale for Black Woman Voices"

How much of this truth can I bear
to see
and still live
unblinded?
How much of this pain can I use?

Reading this, I think, writing is also home, a sometimes-broken home that we are trying to put back together again, but still a home nonetheless.

Every time Mira finds herself in a new situation, I can't help but remember when she was eleven years old at a friend's birthday party, where she tried to sit next to another girl. The girl turned to her and shouted very loudly "No!" Mira limped over to where I was sitting, looking heartbroken. My reaction in that moment was cowardly. I put my arms around her and asked if she wanted to go home. Thankfully, she wanted to stay. Eventually Mira found some other friends and enjoyed herself. At the end of the party, the birthday girl's parents lit some sky lanterns that were supposed to float above the bay behind their home and glide away from the shore, towards the sunset. Thick, gloomy clouds blocked the sunset and most of the lanterns turned to ash, never leaving the ground. Had we left the party, Mira might have learned that someone's

rudeness can send you running home. She also would have missed out on an opportunity to discover, or rediscover, that though home can be a safe place, we shouldn't always rush there.

When I ask Mira what she's writing for Ms. Cardwell's class, she demurs, then tells me that her first piece is about a tree she and her friends used to love to sit under during recess in elementary school.

"The same tree where a boy hit you in the forehead with a rock?" I ask.

. . . .

We are all, writers and non-writers alike, searching for the right words to describe our unique personal state, as well as the overall human condition.

"I'm not going to write about that," she says.

She will be writing about digging for worms under that tree with her girlfriends, she says, most of whom now go to different schools, and have different friends. Like all of her writing, I won't be allowed to read it. This has been our rule since even elementary school. Writing is her home too.

Once while driving Mira home from that same school, we were listening to an audio version of Tillie Olsen's "I Stand Here Ironing" (1956), a short story about a mother discussing her troubled teenage daughter on the phone. I can never revisit that story without thinking of my Haitian mother and all the ironing she did in her bedroom on Sunday nights,

first in our crowded two-room apartment in Port-au-Prince, and later in the two-bedroom apartment my parents rented in East Flatbush and the house they later bought in that part of Brooklyn. When Olsen's character speaks of having to send her daughter away, first to family members, then to a girls' group home, and of the daughter's ensuing separation anxiety, I always feel a lump in my throat. In the car with Mira that day was the first time I was hearing that story as a mother, and in the presence of one of my two daughters.

At the end of the story, I turned to look at Mira in the back seat, and tears were streaming down her face. Overeager and excited, and still being a writer, I asked Mira what exactly about the story was making her cry. Which part moved her? Was it the daughter not being able to keep her mother's letters, or any other personal possessions, with her in the group home? Or was it the final line of the story

where the mother wants her daughter to know that the daughter is "more than this dress on the ironing-board, helpless before the iron"?

After I pushed a bit too much, Mira answered, "I think I cried because you were crying."

Midway through the essay class, while going through a box of old things, I find a wooden machete my mother gave me a few years before she died, a memento she'd bought on a Caribbean cruise. I tell Mira that I am writing about my mother's wooden machete. I tell her that I see the machete as a symbol of the kind of strength that will help us all survive these challenging times. I am also writing about the time when Mira was six years old and we took my mother to the airport so she could return to her home in Brooklyn, after a visit with us in Miami. Taking my mother to the airport and watching her leave always reminded me of my first concrete childhood memory, which was of being peeled off my mother's body on the day she left Haiti for the United States when I was four years old, leaving me in the care of my aunt and uncle in Port-au-Prince for eight years.

. . . .

Stories will remain our transit points, our shorelines, and our home.

That day as Mira and I watched my mother merge into the crowd heading towards her gate at the Miami airport, Mira screamed *"Manman!"* at the top of her voice. My mother turned around and stared at us. She seemed relieved that there was nothing wrong with either Mira or me. As other travelers were dashing around her, my mother took a few steps in our direction, then stopped. She seemed to want to walk back to us, but knew she could not. Coming back to us would mean just postponing another goodbye. Her life, at that time, was in New York, as were her house, her friends, and her church. Her flight was already boarding. She slowly raised the hand that had been resting on her carry-on bag and waved once more, then she turned around and continued walking to her gate.

I ask Mira if she remembers what happened that day. She remembers us taking my mother to the airport a bunch of times, she says, but does not remember ever calling after her. But she does recall another moment at the same place. Once, while my family and I were waiting to board a flight to New York with my mother, my mother went to look for a restroom and accidentally walked past security, leaving the boarding area without her boarding pass

or her cell phone. When our plane began boarding, Mira and I went looking for her and found her pleading, in her somewhat hesitant English, with an impatient TSA officer to let her back in, or at least to accompany her to the gate, and to us.

"She looked so lost and so scared," Mira remembers. "Like she thought she'd never see us again."

I had also feared that we might never see my mother again, or that she might end up on the wrong flight to some distant country, or as an eternal ghost in the airport, passing everyone by. The words my mother would later use to recount to her friends the experience of being lost in the airport now trickle back into my mind. They still sound like the elevator pitch of a much more elaborate four-act tale:

> *M pèdi. Yo jwenn mwen. Vwayaj la kontinye. Nou rive lakay.*
> I am lost. They find me. The journey continues. We arrive home.

"Perhaps home is not a place but simply an irrevocable condition," James Baldwin wrote in his 1956 novel *Giovanni's Room*. Recalling my mother's words, and imagining my daughter's, I know that we have all built a kind of home that no physical separation can take away. In the beginning was the Word, after all, as I suspect it shall also be in the end: stories will remain our transit points, our shorelines, and our home. ✈

The Quest for Home

SANTIAGO RAMOS

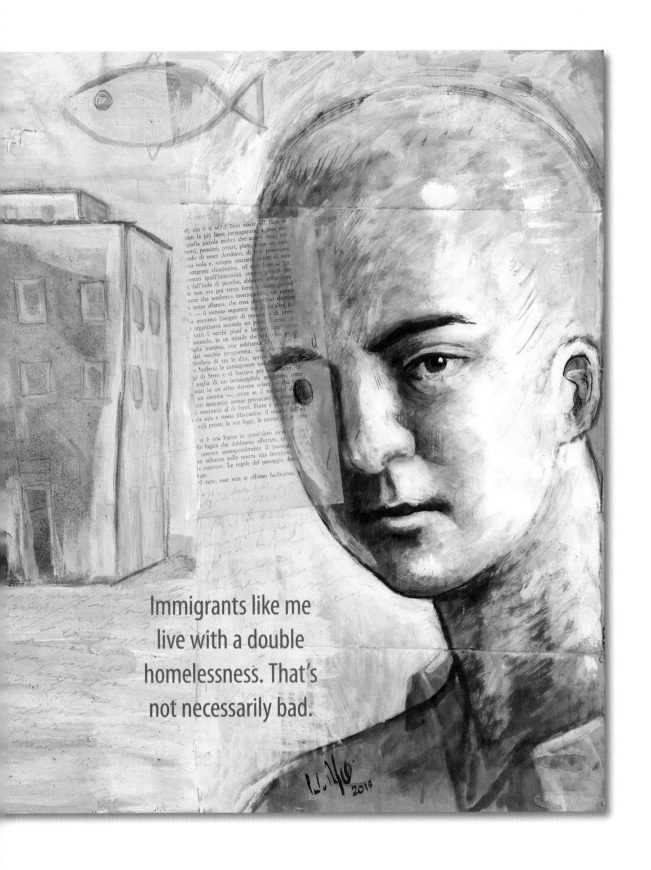

Immigrants like me
live with a double
homelessness. That's
not necessarily bad.

Artwork by Paolo Beneforti. Used by permission from the artist.

Previous spread:
Paolo Beneforti,
Fictional Home,
tempera on
recycled card-
board, 2015

WAS SIX YEARS OLD the first time I crossed a border. I was not an immigrant, exactly, though I would eventually become one. In 1991, my father had obtained a scholarship to attend graduate school at the University of Kansas. Friends told him that completing a doctorate would take five or more years. My mother said that this new country would not become our permanent residence, though we would be there a long time. It was not our home, she said, but we should try to "make ourselves at home."

At that point I had barely come to know my first home – Paraguay, where I was born. Sometimes referred to as a "dark" or "lost" corner of the Americas, the Republic of Paraguay is a landlocked nation in the heart of South America, a subtropical country of grassy plateaus, arid plains, vast marshes, and wooded hills between three great rivers. One, the Pilcomayo, has in recent years shrunk, drying up in parts and devastating the local fauna; the other two – the Paraná and the Paraguay – are so wide that at places they almost seem to disappear into the horizon. About the size of California, with roughly the GDP of Wyoming, Paraguay has around a million fewer inhabitants than New York City. Most of its inhabitants still speak the majority Indigenous language, Guaraní, and many prefer it over Spanish (both are official languages). The country's history is reminiscent of that of Ireland or Poland: like Ireland, Paraguay was subject to colonial rule; like Poland, it is a relatively small country whose independence was more than once imperiled by its bigger and stronger neighbors. And like those European nations, in the furnace of its national struggle it forged a legend ripe with heroes and poets.

I didn't know much about this at age six, however. Most of what I knew back then was a child's inventory of essential shapes, colors, textures, tastes, and sounds. I remembered my grandmother's garden, with its mango tree, crotons, and palms. I could recall the sand-swept, yellow cathedral in the capital city of Asunción. I held on to the smell of sulfur and leaded gasoline in the streets. I never forgot the taste of beef cooked in the *asado* style, and the starchy, cheesy pancakes called *mbeju*. I could picture the gray rubble I saw after a military coup. But after a few years of getting used to what I took to be the world, I was parachuted into a wholly new one: the United States of America. My senses would have to adjust.

Paraguay had been a place with blood-red, sun-cracked soil and flat, wide blades of grass. In the United States, the grass blades were greener, skinnier, perpendicular to the ground, and they lived in front lawns that were trim, with moist brown earth. The people there growled their *r*'s. I had been briefed by my elders. The United States was the wealthy nation where cartoons came from, a place with no soccer. Its people practiced a strange religion – it was called *protestante*, and I was told it was like the Catholic church but "without priests."

I was afraid of this new world. I developed a defense mechanism: I became critical and cocky. On my first evening in the United States, my aunt took me to McDonald's – this was the early 1990s, before McDonald's ventured into South America, but somehow I already knew about Happy Meals and the colorful plastic ball pit, and I had dreamed of one day enjoying both. In the ball pit, I corrected an American boy on his pronunciation: it's *super-MAHN*, of

---

Santiago Ramos is a teacher and writer who grew up in Paraguay and Kansas and currently teaches philosophy at Rockhurst University. His writing has appeared in Commonweal, America, First Things, Image Journal, Salon, *and the Kansas City alt-weekly,* The Pitch.

course. Did I really believe that "Superman" was a Spanish name? For some reason, I held this particular piece of intellectual property to be *mine*, not America's.

Later that year, after we settled into our new house, my mother bought me a collection of school-themed plastic cups. One pictured a series of pencils, pens, and erasers, austerely standing side by side in orderly fashion. Another bore the image of happily personi-fied pencils, pens, and erasers, each laughing and dancing and having a good time. I told my mom: Americans are like the former, Paraguayans are like the latter. How did a six-year-old come to have such a negative view of American society? At some point I had gotten the idea – probably via television, or overheard adult conversations – that the real America was a conformist dystopia, a vast shopping mall, an endless array of blank prefabricated houses, a society cold like air conditioning in July.

This negative view was mostly not informed by real-world observations. It was founded on my feeling of homelessness, a dizziness that can make you adopt a dark interpretation of everything around you. And what I didn't know about, at six, were the proper place names, the neighborhoods, and the beautiful things that make this country a home to its people: tailgating, rodeos, country fairs, jazz, hip hop, baseball, regional cuisines, or the Apollo 11 mission. It would be almost a year before I was able to join the neighborhood kids in lighting sparklers and blowing up firecrackers on Fourth of July weekend. It took a while, but eventually I was able to make myself at home.

One moment of cockiness still nags at my conscience. A few months after the move, I was enrolled in a public school – a decent place that had an English as a Second Language program for students like me. I quickly picked up rudi-mentary English, as most young transplants do. My homeroom teacher, Mrs. Anderson, was the picture of Midwestern warmth and politeness. But for some reason, I disliked Mrs. Anderson's teaching assistant – a woman who must have been in her twenties, working her first teaching job. I misinterpreted some cues, as even kids without a culture barrier can, and I judged her to be an arrogant and patron-izing person. One day, right before the semester winter break, she asked me: "Do you celebrate Christmas?"

I rolled my eyes. "Yes," I said, "I am not *stupid*."

Why did I snap? Because I took her question to be a snooty remark. It established a distance between her and me, her country and my own. *Of course, we celebrate Christmas – we are civilized too, you know.* I was not aware that non-Christian religions existed. But even if her question wounded me, it was also an outstretched hand, though I didn't know it. What might have been a bridge between us – the fact that we both celebrated Christmas – had become a wedge, a border.

> When I returned to Paraguay, the place of my birth had become a foreign country.

FIVE YEARS LATER, I returned to Paraguay. But I did not return home. The place of my birth had become a foreign country, just as foreign to me as the United States had been a few years before. I revisited the old sensory inventory, the ancient experiences of my early childhood, and I felt something akin to an out-of-body experience. The sights and sounds felt familiar, but they felt like the memories of somebody who was not me. I was not the same boy who had played beneath my grandmother's mango tree. The flat grass and the sulfur in the air made me feel uncomfortable – in fact, the polluted air of Asunción for a while made me sick with allergies and asthma.

Now, I was picking up on new, strange details of daily life. In America, milk came in plastic jugs; in Paraguay, it was stored in plastic bags. The spiral notebooks of my Kansas elementary school were replaced by small, hardback notebooks in which we were expected to write in very small print, not the large, loopy letters that were fine for Mrs. Anderson's class. I became obsessed with asphalt – Paraguay seemed to have so little of it – and I made a mental list of all the alternative ways in which streets were paved in Asunción: cobblestone, tile, cement.

But it was the martial culture of Paraguay – a culture that today, after almost two decades of what has been called "globalization," has largely disappeared – that most confused me. It was more than a strange sensory detail; it was a new moral universe. Every morning in my strict private school, we lined up like soldiers getting ready for combat. On Mondays, the school principal inspected us like a general, critiquing any crooked tie or untucked shirt, and took great pains to make his students enunciate every syllable of the national anthem properly and with reverence. We rose from our desks whenever the teacher entered the classroom, and greeted him in unison, barking out: "Good morning, professor!" Those hardback notebooks were meant to be filled with dictations – which I took to mean that the teacher was commanding us exactly what to think. In the school library, the books were kept behind glass, under lock and key.

I rebelled against this culture, just as I had rebelled against the American one. Eventually, my parents found a more "modern," "Americanized" school for me to attend. But I now saw myself as homeless twice over. Today, I can see that the things I experienced back then as "Paraguayan" or "American" do not define the essence of either place; they are merely the things that stood out in the eyes of a child. What made them meaningful was that

they represented two radically distinct places, equally weird to me at the time.

At this point, it became easy for me to feel odd, to focus too much on myself, and to develop a youthful narcissism. An immigrant might avoid this by becoming rooted in a diaspora community, or fully embracing his new nation. But often one goes for both options simultaneously, feeling tugged in both directions, with varying degrees of loyalty to each. And so, the sense of homelessness continues in a different form. That, at least, is what happened to me.

V. S. Naipaul captures this feeling of double homelessness in his 1971 book, *In a Free State*, structured as a series of narratives of twentieth-century displacement. The novel concerns two Europeans from the sheltered world of diplomacy and NGOs during a politically tumultuous period in an unnamed East African nation. The supporting narratives, on the other hand, focus on protagonists from former British colonies, who have migrated to an imperial capital. The main character in "One Out of Many," the first of these stories, opens by comparing both sides of the border he has crossed:

> I am now an American citizen and I live in Washington, capital of the world. Many people, both here and in India, will feel that I have done well. But.
>
> I was so happy in Bombay. I was respected, I had a certain position. I worked for an important man. The highest in the land came to our bachelor chambers and enjoyed my food and showered compliments on me. I also had my friends. We met in the evenings on the pavement below the gallery of our chambers. Some of us, like the tailor's bearer and myself, were domestics who lived in the street. The others were people who came to that bit of pavement to sleep.

Respectable people; we didn't encourage riff-raff. . . . Except of course during the monsoon, I preferred to sleep on the pavement with my friends, although in our chambers a whole cupboard below the staircase was reserved for my personal use.

The irony in this passage is easy to spot: Santosh, the narrator, is obviously giving a somewhat rosy picture of his life in Bombay. His social status had not been an elevated one; he was a servant, and the few luxuries he enjoyed had come from the largesse of his employer. Another source of pride is more questionable, because it is derived from feelings of superiority before the "riff-raff," the lumpen who live in the streets. Despite his fond memories, Santosh had a difficult life, at least by American standards. But he was happy because his place in the world was secure, he could take pride in his work, and he admired the man he worked for. After his boss takes him to the United States, where he has been posted for a government job, Santosh's story begins.

Santosh never fully enjoys his life in Washington. But he cannot fathom returning to Bombay. "I had looked in the mirror and seen myself, and I knew it wasn't possible for me to return to Bombay and to the sort of job I had had and the life I had lived. I couldn't easily become part of someone else's presence again." The only life left to him is the life of

commerce – he manages to make a good living as a cook in an Indian restaurant. But success in business doesn't produce the feeling of belonging that he once had. By now, Santosh has abandoned any hope of finding something called "home." This concept has been replaced by a stripped-down, abstract view of human life: "All that my freedom has brought me is the knowledge that I have a face and have a body, that I must feed this body and clothe this body for a certain number of years. Then it will be over."

Naipaul's story depicts an extreme case, and in many ways, Santosh is a bad character. But through this story, Naipaul recognizes an illuminating, often painful, moment in an immigrant's story: the dawning of a feeling of homelessness combined with a constant, unshakable yearning for home.

Paolo Beneforti, *The City,* tempera and marker on recycled cardboard, 2015

forget those things I loved about Paraguay, as quickly as possible. I also tried to make myself feel important: Maybe there was something noble and modern in not having a fixed place in the world. I hadn't read *In a Free State* yet, but I could have been convinced that Santosh's bare-bones anthropology is the truth of the human condition. Home is an illusion, I told myself, a collection of comforting and familiar sensations and memories, but we don't *really* belong anywhere. A version of this belief, one could argue, is even part of the Christian tradition: Didn't Thérèse of Lisieux, the French Catholic mystic, say: "The world is thy ship and not thy home"? Moreover, the question of home seemed tied to the idea of nationhood, a concept with, at best, a fading reputation. Once you've crossed a border – it seemed to me then – you discover that we are all, ultimately, homeless.

Writing about *In a Free State*, the novelist Neel Mukherjee argues that the legacy of Naipaul's work should be the development of an aesthetic that eschews the very idea of home, that embraces the idea that a human being can be fulfilled and still be homeless. "I'm envisaging a novel which sees outsiderness as enabling, a form that has at its center the question, 'What is our place in the world?' and is unafraid not only to question the whole notion of place but also to return another unflinching question: 'Why must we have a place in the world?'"

When I moved back to the United States a second time, in my late teens, I would have found it tempting to answer that question by saying we don't in fact need one. Moving a third time was painful, but I developed a new defense mechanism: since the pain I felt was driven by my attachment to home, I tried to

BUT WHAT DO WE even mean by "home"? Those who search for it are on "a quest for peace, justice, and community," writes Emmy Barth in *No Lasting Home: A Year in the Paraguayan Wilderness*, an account of the Bruderhof community's journey from England to their establishment in Paraguay. Their journey of uprooting, exile, and making a stable life beyond borders cuts a hopeful contrast to the despair in Naipaul's story.

In the 1930s, the still-young Bruderhof community, pacifist and drawing members from various European countries, refused to render homage to Hitler. They had been surveilled by the regime since at least 1933. Eventually, they fled to England. But England proved to be something less than hospitable – the German roots of the movement, along with its unwillingness to contribute to the war effort, made the Bruderhof suspect in the eyes of many British people.

Their unlikely next stop was Paraguay. As far as the Bruderhof were concerned, the country had a few advantages. A community of Mennonites had already been living there since 1927, and the Bruderhof had joined the Mennonite World Conference in 1936. *Los menonitas*, as they are called by the rest of Paraguay, are a well-known community there, though mostly out of sight – their largest dwelling, the far-off western city of Filadelfia, is a difficult six-hour drive from the capital. (As a child, I only knew that they produced milk and were *protestantes*. I never wondered whether they celebrated Christmas.)

The Paraguayan government, writes Barth, offered the Bruderhof the same privileges it had offered the Mennonites: "Freedom of religion, freedom to run their own schools, and exemption from military service." Finally, Paraguay was (still is) sparsely populated, with a lot of open land, although letters from the Bruderhof members also show an acquaintance with the "so-called Indians from whom the land had been stolen" – that is, the previously displaced Guarani Ñandeva, Ayoreo, and other Indigenous peoples. When they arrived in Paraguay, the Bruderhof spent the first few months living in the Mennonite settlements.

When the Mennonites arrived in 1927, Paraguay was living through a long period led by the Liberal Party, when elegant and somewhat despotic European-educated elites ruled the country with a combination of laissez-faire capitalism and Beaux-Arts aesthetics (the nicest buildings and piazzas in Asunción are

from this era). It was not an altogether democratic era – officials fixed elections, imposed curfews, clamped down on protests – but it was a time when, to a greater or lesser degree, the nation's leaders subscribed to high-minded principles, such as the freedom of religion that both the Mennonites and the Bruderhof found crucial for their survival.

The Bruderhof group arrived in 1940, however, at a pivotal moment. Paraguay would soon undergo changes that, while not immediately affecting the government's open policy toward European Protestant refugees, greatly altered the political climate in other ways. In 1935 Paraguay had triumphed over Bolivia in the war over the Chaco region – the very region where the Mennonites had settled, and where the Bruderhof hoped to find a home. The war boosted Paraguayan nationalism, and the generation that fought it became part of patriotic lore the way the "greatest generation" did later in the United States. That victory, however, also meant the demise of the Liberal era.

After a coup early in 1936, the Paraguayan military, which was given the lion's share of credit for victory in the Chaco, became the de facto executive of the nation, effectively holding electoral veto power. Even worse, during the 1930s the military had become enthralled by the style of the *Wehrmacht*, whose exploits were celebrated by thousands of Nazi-sympathizing German nationals living in Paraguay at the time (along with some Paraguayan elites). This connection was only one of the Nazi-related ironies that the Bruderhof encountered upon arriving in Paraguay. It is unclear, reading Barth's account, whether the Mennonites who supported Hitler (about half) did so because they believed in his ideology, or due to the misguided idea that he defended "Christian values." Certainly many believed that he might rebuild Germany into a place more hospitable to Christians, away from the anti-religious influence of the Communists. The Bruderhof tried to persuade these Mennonites that these views were wrong – in their words, *Lieber Hakenwurm als Hakenkreuz*: better hookworms than swastikas.

Hookworms are still pretty bad, though; they burrow into your foot and can cause serious disease, the ailment known to Paraguayans as the *ceboí*, which like most people I was warned about as a kid. And there were plenty of other drawbacks in the Chaco: there was malaria and drought and strange lizards. To this day, the Chaco remains a forbidding place to live. Cotton grew well there, but that was about it: food was often scarce. At the time, the Mennonites themselves seemed spiritually depleted by the struggle to survive. The Bruderhof's new home was anything but a land of milk and honey.

An increasingly difficult situation was resolved, for the Bruderhof, when they purchased land in eastern Paraguay – a lusher, more fertile region. There they founded a colony named Primavera, "springtime." In their farewell message to the Mennonites they articulated an attitude that reconciles home and homelessness:

> Unless you understand our community, it may not be so easy to understand why we have decided to leave the Chaco. The main reason is a spiritual one. . . . We want to be close to other people because we have a message to bring them. . . . We cannot hide behind a wall – or a desert – and say, "We don't want the world to touch us!" The world is within us. And there is a danger that a group withdraws into itself and is concerned only for its own blessedness and its own economy. Our task as Christians is a missionary one.

The home that they wanted was one that stretched beyond its own borders in service. It is moving to read the story of a people who found a home in the very home you yourself once had to leave. And it's striking to consider the chance that my great-grandfather, who worked in the port of Asunción, and was himself an immigrant from the Canary Islands, may have witnessed the arrival of the Bruderhof in 1940. If he rose from his desk and spied the European refugees walking along the boardwalk, did he see himself in them – who spoke a different language and worshiped in a different church, but who underwent the same painful process of uprooting that he himself had gone through? Today, in my thirties, having also moved around several times within the United States, I feel American, but since I was six years old, I have not felt fully "at home." Do the formerly border-hopping Bruderhof members now feel Paraguayan?

From their story, I have gleaned a response to the quandary of double homelessness. First, never give up on the desire for a home; that desire fuels life itself. It was instrumental for the Bruderhof's survival, and their ultimate deliverance. Second, there is no *permanent* home. In a sense, the most stable home the Bruderhof had was each other – the portable home of their own community, which nevertheless required a place in which to settle down. Those two points yield an unavoidable conclusion: Our task is always to try to build a home – a place of peace, justice, and community – and to extend the greatest possible compassion to those who cross borders in search of one. There is no earthly home – Thérèse was right. But the longing to discover and build an eternal one begins in this life. ⤳

There is no earthly home. But the longing to discover and build an eternal one begins in this life.

Eyvind Earle,
Jeweled Trees,
oil, 1999

The Hunger Winter, 1944–5
(*The Netherlands*)

A dark, dictated famine made by war.
Small fires, for warmth, lit up the towns; canals
blockaded by command froze up, as if
to make a point. The Dutch began to starve.
They gnawed on sugar beets and tulip bulbs.

Out walking here, in Naarden's ancient woods,
I see a stand of trees made strange by war.
Bullets have signed the bark, their wounds a mad
and modern *furioso.* No Arden here.
And in the rows of trees, a few grow straight
but only for a foot or two, then veer
off east or west, continuing to rise
within a different column of air as if
an origami fold had given them
a surreal twist. These trees were cut for fuel
but over seven decades grew again.
Time is simple for a tree, it hides
its rings inside, a strange geometry
by which a rise inscribes itself as round.
The reckoning of feet or yards remains
visible, as though the tree might be
a giant wooden ruler marking years.
These limping trees look frightened, almost as if,
having seen something terrible, they tried
to take a step—they tried to walk, or run.
Three-quarters of a century is long,
even if less long for trees, which hold
their winters close, and imperceptibly, rise.
They never will grow straight now, yet they grow.

SUSAN DE SOLA

Blue Star Line de Luxe Mail Service to South America   T.S.S. "Andalucia"

Refugee Letters

At the height of World War II, three women flee Europe with their community for a pioneer life in South America.

EMMY BARTH MAENDEL

TRAUTEL GROANED and stumbled dizzily back to her bed, fighting nausea as the ship rolled under her feet. In his nearby basket, her baby stirred. Felix was only five weeks old and had cried most of the night. He was quiet now, but she herself could not sleep. What lay ahead for her little one? "God, why are you leading us into the danger-ridden tropics? What sacrifices will be demanded of us?" She remembered the fear that had clutched her heart in Liverpool as she crossed the gangplank onto the ship, little Felix held tight in her arms. She felt that the fates of all of them were on a razor's edge, suspended between life and death, heaven and earth. "Will I ever touch solid ground again? Will the demon of war let this big ship pass unscathed?" She pulled herself together. "Do not question, my soul, but trust. God is leading us out of a war-torn country. He will protect us and our children on the ocean and also in the strange land we are traveling to."

Emmy Barth Maendel is a member of the Bruderhof communities and the author of several books including No Lasting Home: A Year in the Paraguayan Wilderness *(Plough), from which this article is adapted.*

It was the end of November 1940. They were on a luxury liner, the *Andalucia Star,* one of the few passenger ships to dare the submarine-infested ocean. It had no second-class berths, so the eighty refugees she was crossing with traveled first-class.

Leo and Trautel Dreher had left Switzerland eleven years earlier to join the Bruderhof, a Christian community then located in Germany. Little could they have known what taking this step would mean: that they would soon have to flee Nazi Germany for England, and then England, too, for the sake of their pacifist convictions. Now, with six small children, they were on their way to Paraguay, that mysterious, landlocked little country in the middle of South America.

Marianne Zimmermann was on the ship, too, with her husband, Kurt, and their four children. She kept a journal for them to read when they grew up:

> With this voyage, a new period of our community's history begins. We've taken leave of a beautiful home and are now preparing for a new life. I would like to write something for you, my beloved children, about this trip, which will have great significance. The goal, the castle and the city in which Jesus lives, is and remains the same, even if there are many unknown paths before us. We must look unwaveringly to Jesus; Peter was able to walk safely on the water as long as he looked to Jesus.

Phyllis Rabbitts, a thirty-four-year-old English nurse and midwife who had come to the community only a few months earlier, wrote a letter to her family describing the departure:

> The idea of a whole community being transferred from one country to another in wartime was something one could not grasp. It seemed too great a miracle. We had realized for many months the insecurity of our position in England as there was so much hate growing in the hearts of the general populace. This could be understood because we had many German members; also the pacifism of our English members roused a bitter spirit in nationalistic minds.

> Although national and local government officials were tolerant and understanding, our economic position was getting acute because of the local hostility, which crippled our business. Also the curfew affecting our "alien" members curtailed considerably our sending out brothers for mission. The church was in peril and had to be saved, and there was a definite leading from God that we should leave the country.

> Following this leading from God was not easy. We had a well built-up Bruderhof – the dwelling houses were still quite new, and the dining/meeting room was brand new and beautiful in its simplicity. The laundry with its modern machines had also not long been set in motion and was a tremendous boon to those who had known what it was to wash everything by hand in difficult conditions. The new baths and toilets were also a very welcome achievement. In fact, all over the whole Bruderhof one could see the fruits of four to five years' struggle and hard labor.

> But now the time had come to lay down our tools and leave all this and to pick them up again in another country that we could not choose for ourselves.

> Having so many young children and several elderly and infirm members, all this was far from easy, for no one could foresee this kind of journey in wartime. Twenty-two babies were born in the year 1940 (one was stillborn) and twenty in the previous year, so there were many very young children taken to Paraguay.

> After a long seeking and waiting to know the will of God concerning us, the

Operated by England's Blue Star Line, the *Andalucia Star,* which carried Bruderhof refugees across the Atlantic in 1940, was torpedoed off West Africa two years later.

first group left the Cotswold Bruderhof to build up afresh in a hitherto unknown (to us) land – the Chaco region of Paraguay! . . . Between there and England lay the dangerous ocean, where ships were being either sunk or bombed almost daily. . . .

For what purpose were we being led out of England to Paraguay? Many such questions filled our thoughts. But deep down in our hearts was a strong feeling that . . . together we would continue the fight and struggle so that God's will might be done through us, wherever that might be.

> **"Between Paraguay and England lay the dangerous ocean, where ships were being either sunk or bombed almost daily."**
>
> Phyllis Rabbitts

The *Andalucia Star* steamed down the South American coast, stopping now and then at various ports, until it entered the Río de la Plata.

A Brazilian doctor boarded and examined everyone. Three days later – four days before Christmas 1940 – they left the luxurious ocean liner that had been their home for four weeks. They boarded a steamboat that was to take them up the Paraná River, deep into the South American interior.

From now on there were no more first-class comforts. They were traveling third class, all eighty-one of them, in one large room in the hold of the ship, with no windows. Each adult shared a bed with a child. The heat was intense, the stench terrible, and the cabin dirty; Cyril Davies, the community's doctor, forbade drinking water without boiling it first. During the day they sat among the bags and trunks, trying to distract the children with songs and games. Marianne wrote:

Now we were really entering the unknown! In spite of the terrible heat, in spite of the cramped quarters and dirt and loudly screaming passengers, we felt more comfortable, more that we were "on the road," on the path of the pioneers. For young people without children, the whole trip would have been an adventure. But to care for our little children was not easy, especially regarding hygiene. We bathed them in barrels that were filled with river water and in which we also washed our laundry. Many children got heat rash or other rashes.

It was Christmas Day when the steamer arrived in Asunción, the Paraguayan capital. Paraíso trees were in bloom along the streets. The heat was oppressive to the northern European newcomers. They changed boats again, getting into a small barge with only a canvas cover for shelter. First the luggage was transferred – all twenty-three tons. After that, there was no room left, and the people sat squashed between their bags. The children were crying; several had fevers. Again they were to sleep in the windowless hold, but this time they got several first-class cabins for the sick and the pregnant women. They ate bananas and pineapples, as other food was hard to procure.

They watched the riverbanks closely, trying to envision these unfamiliar surroundings as their new home – mile after mile of largely uncultivated land, shrubs, and palm trees. Dark herons and snowy egrets stood amid the marsh grasses; flocks of parrots and a few toucans flew overhead. One day the children crowded to the rail to see a crocodile. A hot wind blew in from the shore, laden with the scent of orange blossoms. Sometimes the boat docked at small port towns, and Paraguayans and Indigenous women could be seen, carrying large baskets of bananas or *chipa*, a local bread, on their heads.

After two days' travel they arrived in Puerto Casado, the river port that marked the end of this part of their journey. Marianne found that all three of her young daughters had contracted lice on the riverboat. She withdrew with them into a corner and began combing out their hair. "At least we are here together, alive and healthy," she comforted herself in her diary.

N THE CHACO, the arid region of western Paraguay, Marianne and her fellow immigrants found a temporary home in a colony of Mennonites, who housed them in their school. Marianne spent her days supervising the thirteen school-age children. Excursions through the thorny underbrush offered exciting discoveries – fossilized seashells in the sand, remnants of the prehistoric sea, brilliantly colored butterflies, and a bounty of birds. There were vultures and parrots, wild pigeons, and even a small woodpecker with a bright red head. The wild animals were shy, but not the snakes, which came uncomfortably close to the community's shelters.

The narrow paths trodden by the Indigenous local people yielded new surprises too. Once the children came across a woman sitting on the ground in a little clearing, weaving. Holding the threads taut with her big toe, she skillfully wove them into bracelets, necklaces, and belts.

The community sent out search parties to look for land where they could settle. As one of their leaders, Hans Meier, later reported:

> Some of us started out with a Lengua (Enlhet) chief to find a place. We deliberately turned not only to the company that owned the land, but also to the so-called Indians from whom the land had been stolen. They were very helpful because they understood our longing for community. After riding for several hours on small horses – instead

Top to bottom: Trautel Dreher with her children at the Cotswold Bruderhof in England, 1937; the Atlantic crossing on the *Andalucia Star,* 1940; Phyllis Rabbitts, 1940; Boarding a steamboat for the inland journey; Kurt and Marianne Zimmermann with their children in Paraguay, 1941.

Carretas, or ox carts, were a common mode of transportation among the Paraguayan communities. Woodcut by Victor Crawley, a Bruderhof member, ca. 1950.

game from their hunting expeditions or whatever they earned to the oldest woman, who divided and distributed it according to need.

In the end, the property they bought was in the east part of Paraguay, in a sparsely populated area of mixed savannah and jungle with more rainfall that promised to be easier to farm. After three months in their makeshift quarters, the group piled their families onto wagons for another move. The new place was a ranch called Primavera – "spring."

As they bumped through the forest, the pioneers admired the palm trees and the wide view of green meadows edged by dark woods. Finally they saw the thatched roofs of Primavera – houses that an advance group had quickly constructed as their new home. Marianne wrote a few weeks later:

> We have now been here for a good month, in Primavera, at Isla Margarita, the highest point, more or less in the middle of our property. Day by day it becomes more of a "Bruderhof." There are many palms up here, signs of the peace of the city on the hill that is to arise here. May it truly become a fortress of Zion! God has led us into a beautiful land. In every respect this is a unique and wonderful time, where besides the joy and strain of building, the church will have to be newly founded inwardly. I have yearned for a long time that for once everything in the church might become new, like at the beginning, through a refreshing spirit, a Pentecost that will make us all new from the bottom up. God has led his weak, little flock together in such a wonderful way, one group after the other. But it becomes ever clearer to me that this will be given to us only insofar as we accept the way of Christ. We will have to suffer and

of saddles, we rode on sheepskins – we arrived at a large tract of land which the chief indicated would be a good place for us to settle. As the formal purchase price for the property, which was comprised of several hundred hectares, he asked for only one dollar. Instead of a signed contract, he requested a handshake, which was of more value to him than a written statement.

Accompanying him to his home after this, we found a tree, the lowest branches of which were covered to keep the rain off. All the members of his community sat on the ground in a circle around this tree. Apparently it was here that they handed in the

Plough Quarterly • *Autumn 2021*

will be allowed to suffer; we must surrender and will be allowed to surrender ourselves completely; we shall pass through death, believing and expecting that the kingdom of God is near.

They lived in the "Gallop Hut," so named for the speed with which it had been erected. It consisted of a corrugated iron roof on palm trunk supports. Four "halls" were still being built. These had thatched roofs on wooden posts sunk one meter into the ground. Neither the Gallop Hut nor the halls had walls to separate families. People used their luggage and mosquito nets to give an illusion of privacy and dressed before it got light. Phyllis described their living conditions in a letter to her family in England:

> Sometimes we get very heavy dews in the mornings, and anything that is not under cover is very wet. As we have no walls to our houses, it penetrates everywhere. We have no furniture yet so live in our trunks, so to speak, and that is not too easy. When they have been packed tightly to come, things don't go back so easily. It is a real camp life for us all. We all sleep on bedsteads but no mattresses, and when there aren't enough bedsteads, and there often haven't been, people sleep on benches. We are all hardening and it is good. Civilization has become too soft, and comfort takes too high a place in one's life to the detriment of one's inner life. I am very glad to have experienced the poverty and need of these first weeks in Paraguay. I had taken too much for granted in the old life before I came to the Bruderhof. I always thought I would have sheets to sleep in and bread and butter to eat, or at least margarine, and a cup of tea to drink. I never thought that I could eat rice for breakfast, rice for dinner, and rice for supper (and not made with fresh milk, only water and some cheap dried milk). We have little cow's milk, and that the children have. Bread is scarce, but we usually get a little once a day. Even so, I'm told we have better food than when the community was in Germany. I think that there they semi-starved. Actually our chief difficulty is the sicknesses and having no doctor. So many (in fact, nearly all) our people and children have septic wounds on their legs and elsewhere. We are up against a very horrible kind of wound, such as one wouldn't meet in England. Nearly all the wounds have live worms or maggots in them and give much pain. Some of the children have these wounds in their heads and must have their heads shaved. My first experience with this nearly sapped all my courage and made me feel very sick, as I had to extract one from a tiny child's eye. I am nursing sick babies and children all day long.

> "We are all hardening and it is good. Civilization has become too soft, and comfort takes too high a place in one's life to the detriment of one's inner life."
> Phyllis Rabbitts

By June 1941, 329 men, women, and children had made it across the ocean. In addition, seven babies had been born since leaving England. Finally all were together in one location. Would they be able to realize their dream of making Primavera a "city on a hill"? They knew it would take hard physical work; perhaps they did not realize that the spiritual work would be even harder. Phyllis wrote in July:

> One feels one cannot sit still and do nothing while there is so much sorrow and suffering around one; and until he or anyone sees

the need and feels the call to give oneself to a new order he will find himself more and more caught up in the old one. I can only say I hope that this judgment on the earth will be shortened and that mankind will listen and harken to the message which it brings. . . . It is a shocking thing that war is needed to shake one out of oneself into seeing and feeling the need of the whole world; and for some of us it has needed this, but how infinitely more tragic is it if a war, and such a war, fails to do that for us. We must indeed search within ourselves to learn the secret of our deadness and long that light and life shall break in.

> **"We are only ordinary human beings and we couldn't stand any of this if it were not for the strength given us."**
> Phyllis Rabbitts

Over the fall and winter, housing conditions slowly improved, and the men began drawing up plans for a hospital that would serve both the community and their new Paraguayan neighbors.

THE HOSPITAL WASN'T YET FINISHED when, in October, Trautel's eleven-month-old son, Felix, fell sick. One evening when she went to pick him up from the nursery, he was lying in his crib, crying piteously. She was alarmed. He had a loud cough, hard and barking. He seemed to have a fever, and his breathing was quick, with something of a rattle.

It was a restless night. His breathing grew more and more rapid. His chest heaved, his eyes were dull; his arms stretched out listlessly on the blanket. His voice was hoarse when he cried, his lips parched. Through the long night Trautel sat at his side. The community gathered to pray for his life. But the next day, less than twenty-four hours after she noticed he was sick, he died.

Later Trautel wrote in her diary: "O my child, with what pain I bore you! Is it joy or pain that now fills my heart and bosom? I do not know. I only know that I give my child back to God who gave him to me."

Two months later, when the community celebrated Christmas 1941, it was a bittersweet time. They gave thanks for their safe passage across the dangerous ocean and their first year in a new country. Yet their escape from war-wracked Europe had come at a heavy cost: in addition to Felix, four other children had been lost. As Marianne wrote:

> With great thankfulness we left the old year behind and began the new. In the past months God gave so much to the church that our hearts have not really taken it in. One thing stands above all else: God's love and grace and mercy are great and were with us – also in the dark hours of death.

Phyllis confided to her sister back in England: "We are only ordinary human beings and we couldn't stand any of this if it were not for the strength given us to give up all for the sake of Christ and his kingdom of peace and justice. If we lose faith or lack vision, then the whole thing becomes impossible."

All the same, Phyllis had learned to face the practical challenges of her new life with equanimity: "We are thankful to have a roof, and the bits of sacking when a storm comes in all its fury. And they come often. Often one has had one's bed and things wet, and as for the sand, it gets into everything, and then comes the sun again and dries all up, and we wash and make clean again until the next sand comes." ⤳

Yohanan Simon,
*Orange Picking in
the Kibbutz*, 1946

Life in Zion

YANIV SAGEE

A kibbutz veteran calls Zionism back to its founding vision of a shared society.

Yaniv Sagee, a lifelong member of an Israeli kibbutz, is a political activist, a dairy farmer, and a high school teacher. For thirty years he has fought for civil rights for Palestinians and Arab Israelis, and advocates for peace. Plough's *Timothy Keiderling spoke with him about why it's crucial to recover Zionism's roots to build a shared society.*

Plough: Questions about Zionism, about communal living, and about brotherhood between nations – other people can opt into wrestling with them, but you were born into them. Can you tell us about your background?

Yaniv Sagee: I was born in 1963 in Kibbutz Ein HaShofet in northern Israel. True to the original vision of kibbutz living, we shared all things in common: my family had no private property. I grew up in the children's house, where we also slept and had our classes. It was a very good childhood.

Then, when I was seventeen, my father died. He was a Zionist, a Holocaust survivor. His ideals shaped me. His life was a quest for peace and justice for all. And he taught me that we will never have justice and peace if the Palestinians don't also. That has guided me ever since. He also taught me that I needed to be responsible for my community, for our movement: Ein HaShofet was created by the Hashomer Hatzair Youth Movement, started in 1913. It held three values: Zionism, socialism, and brotherhood of people.

What's the connection between those three things? They seem pretty far apart. Israel is a capitalist country; when a lot of people think of Zionism, the brotherhood of all people is the last thing that comes to mind. What would you say to them?

Zionism, for my father and our movement, meant we must take responsibility for the future of the Jewish people, to create a Jewish homeland where we will have shelter from anti-Semitism.

But it wasn't just about having a nation like other nations, a place of safety. It was also meant to be a better place than any other, built on equality and justice. That's where socialism came in. What we meant by socialism was

that all people should live in community, in conditions of legal and material equality. And we wanted to do that without waiting. We wanted to create a new society and jump right to the final stage of socialism. It's not something out there in the future. It was to be built by the movement, there and then, in the land of Israel.

It was so practical, when I was growing up! You don't just speak about things, you actualize them. I started work at age seven, cleaning our children's house, taking care of the children's mini-zoo – we had a zoo to learn to be responsible for animals. If we didn't take care of the animals, they would die. So, we needed to work hard to build this land.

But there were already people in that land.

We believe that the Jewish people need a homeland. We are coming back to Zion because this is the historical and natural homeland of the Jewish people. But we also believe it's possible to live together with the Palestinian people that have been living in this place for so long. Those were the values I learned from my father.

But it hasn't been a straightforward path. What happened after your father died?

I went into the army – everyone has to serve. We have three mandatory years and then serve about one month a year as reserves. As soon as I could, I came back to the kibbutz. Then, at twenty-five, I was elected to serve as general secretary of the kibbutz. It was just for a term – we rotate positions, that's part of our way to live. There should not be the managing class and the simple people. People came to me and I helped them. This is the basic doctrine: we give everything we can, and we receive everything we need.

The kibbutz had put me through Tel Aviv University; once I finished my studies the plan was for me to manage the dairy business, though I wanted to be a teacher at the high school. But what I do – this is not a personal decision. About a year after I got back, people started wanting to make their own decisions professionally. I said, "No, the kibbutz needs to decide where to send me." They tried to tell me that's not how we do things anymore, but I said, "This is my vocation. I am going to be a public servant, so I need the public to decide where I am needed."

So I was the manager of the dairy for one year and then joined the high school as a teacher and educator. By that time I was married, and this service was a part of how I understood what it was to be a husband to Galia, a father to my children. It's not that I'm this big figure running organizations; rather, first I'm taking all the burden of the family on my shoulders. It's our way as a couple. We share the vocation. We find a way so that even when I'm elected to big positions, it always becomes part of the family and the family becomes part of the community.

Later I was elected as the head of our youth movement and after five years as general secretary of the kibbutz. Through that, I started working with the government, and other kibbutzim.

Yohanan Simon, *Watchmen in the Vineyard,* 1950

You've linked the future of the kibbutz movement with what you've called "shared society" and with peace. How are all these things connected to Zionism?

They're all connected, even though they seem to contradict each other. The kibbutz is a Zionist socialist community, but Zionism is about the Jewish people, while socialism is international. For years, Zionism has struggled with these contradictions. As in the State of Israel, so it's been with the kibbutz movement: Zionism has come first. And when Zionism contradicted the brotherhood of people, then the kibbutzniks put brotherhood of people aside. This is a big problem.

Theodor Herzl, in the nineteenth century, called not for a *Jewish state* but a state *for the Jews*, to connect all Jewish people. Herzl understood that the land where we want to come back, Zion, is not empty. Arabs, too, have their homes here.

A century ago, 1921, was the first conflict with the Arab Palestinians, a bloody confrontation in Jaffa. From then on, the question faced us: Would we push to have a Jewish state

Yohanan Simon, *Shabbat on the Kibbutz*, 1947, oil on canvas

Could you say a little about what you think a shared society would look like?

For fifty-four years, Israel has been an occupier in the West Bank. People there, and in Gaza, are living in cruel conditions. Hamas is a bloody terrorist group, but that doesn't change that fact. Israel describes itself as a democratic Zionist Jewish state. We need to decide between the Jewish and democratic natures of the state. Israel must continue to be a homeland of the Jewish people, but also a shared state, where all citizens are equal. To make that work, Palestinian people need to have their own country, with the 1967 borders.

This is what I mean by a shared society – a place that all citizens view as their home. Inside Israel (without the occupied territories) the population is 80 percent Jewish and 20 percent Arab. We must start living together, going to the same schools. We need to have at least 20 percent Arabs in every public institution in Israel. Arabs, like Jews, need to do national service. And we also need to have processes of forgiveness, committees for truth and reconciliation.

It's not so far-fetched! In most places, people feel good about the public sphere. We already share some spaces: go to the big mall in Nazareth, to hospitals, to restaurants, you'll see Arabs and Jews together. Go to Jerusalem and Haifa and see that the notice that the bus will be ten minutes late is in Hebrew and Arabic. This is possible. We will learn how to do this.

What's the place of the kibbutz movement in that shared society?

regardless of how we achieved it, or would we understand that first we needed to settle how we live together with the Arab inhabitants of the country? The movement I'm part of has tried to say, "We need to find a way to live with the Palestinians."

After the Holocaust, it was even more clear than before that we needed a place of safety. And we do! But since then, Zionism became a nationalistic movement, not as focused on the *ideals* of the Jewish people. That's earned us a lot of criticism, including the 1975 UN resolution that Zionism is racism.

Zionism is still needed, but it can't be based on anti-Jewish morals. Zionism needs to come back from its nationalistic approach to become, again, a movement for Jewish people, where our homeland is just one tool in our toolbox for the continuation of the Jewish people.

The kibbutzim were socialist Zionist settlements. What we mean by socialism is what you in the Bruderhof mean by it: each one gives according to his ability and receives according to his needs. No one is alone, everyone is taken care of. For this to work we have to trust each other. We're secular – most kibbutzim are – but we're based on faith in a mission, a purpose beyond simply communal living. That mission, that faith, was that it is our responsibility to create a better world, and at the same time a sustained existence for the Jewish people. We needed to create a better society in Israel, based on justice, which involves partnership with the Arabs. We needed to be agents of peace. And part of this peace is to build Jewish culture – arts, music, literature. The kibbutzim were carrying out this mission. That was a very good system. It worked great; that's why there are 273 kibbutzim all over Israel.

But even by the early 1960s, this began to break down. We lost a sense of vocation. And even vocation is not enough. Another thing I learned from the Bruderhof, which is crucial but which was never a part of the kibbutz movement, is the centrality of forgiveness. The ability to live in an intimate society where you do not have a whole load of negative emotions towards others is essential. And you have a way to practice that, but we never had it.

I used to be a mediator. People would assure me a conflict was over, but we had no way to stop the feelings of hurt and hatred. We have people in the kibbutz hating others because they were hurt years ago. Some carry that to the next generation. You cannot run a community like this. We don't have members with a sense of vocation beyond themselves. And we do not forgive.

Now, most of the kibbutzim are good homes, comfortable places to live. We have waiting lists; there are more kibbutzniks than ever. They all want to come to these privatized kibbutzim. People say it's great. You get a good house. There's good community that functions better than the city. We pay taxes. Good education, good healthcare. People are closer than in the city. It's a nice liberal community, a comfortable suburban home. But it's not going to last. We're running on fumes.

In the past, we would tell people that didn't subscribe to the ideas of the kibbutz, "OK, you don't believe. Go, leave. This is who we are." Now those people tell us, "We are staying. We are stakeholders like you and we are going to change things to suit us." What happened in Ein HaShofet is that I stayed in the kibbutz, but the kibbutz left the kibbutz.

> Zionism is still needed, but it can't be based on anti-Jewish morals.

So what's next? Is there a future?

I feel that the kibbutz is very important, so I am going to try. There needs to be change, but not just a change to privatization. We have to find a new path. We can't rely on getting hold of the past, because it doesn't exist anymore, the people don't carry it in their heart. I believe the kibbutz needs a new model, a model I call a "braided kibbutz." You have different levels of commitment woven together. On the most committed level, you'd have people holding a common purse. At the outer edges would be families living privately. You could choose your level of commitment, and all would be interwoven. There will be a common overarching circle for all.

A shared society, even for people who disagree on what that society means?

Yes, a shared society, based on partnership between differences. ⤙

This article combines three interviews from July 2021, edited for length and clarity.

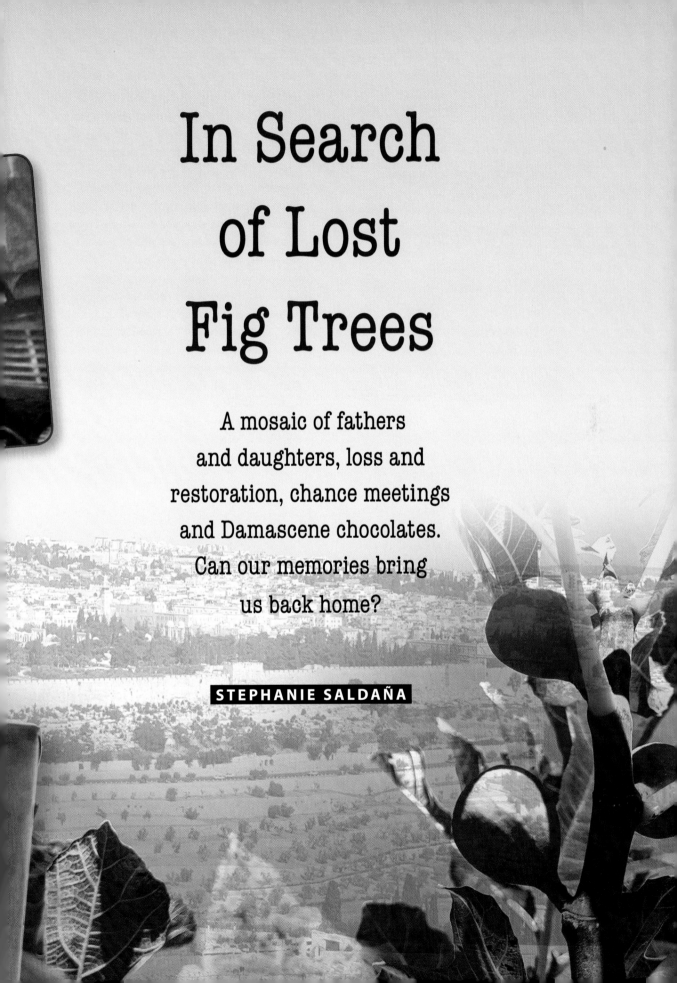

In Search of Lost Fig Trees

A mosaic of fathers
and daughters, loss and
restoration, chance meetings
and Damascene chocolates.
Can our memories bring
us back home?

STEPHANIE SALDAÑA

star." In the following decades, Shihab would reflect on his sense of exile in newspaper articles, a cookbook called *A Taste of Palestine*, and a memoir about his return to be with his mother on her deathbed. Yet he would become most famous as the subject of his daughter's poems. In Naomi Shihab Nye's work he appears over and over again, until he becomes as familiar to us as the gentle pull of her voice. Her father, recounting traditional stories about Joha next to her bedside. Her father, singing Arabic in the shower. Her father, hit by a stone on the head as a boy. Her father, preparing thick Arabic coffee. Her father, calling out for home until the end.

In one of her most famous poems, "My Father and the Fig Tree," Naomi Shihab Nye recounts the story of her father obsessively searching for figs in America, trying to explain their magic, as though the very touch of them might transport him home. She writes:

> For other fruits my father was indifferent.
> He'd point at the cherry trees and say,
> "See those? I wish they were figs."

The children of refugees wrote to Naomi, understanding. She recounts in her introduction to her father's cookbook that the letters would say: "For my father it was a plum tree," or "My father felt exactly that way about a grapefruit tree."

But all this would come later: the books, the letters, the poems. For a moment, let us return to Aziz Shihab's arrival in New York. It is not only a new country: it is as if the world as he has known it has been pulled from beneath his feet. He writes letters home to his mother to tell her that he has safely arrived.

He only learns later that he has been mailing them into trashcan slots.

1/

Previous spread: Nour Al Ghraowi with her father, *top, 1997;* Naomi Shihab Nye with her father, *bottom,* 1956

In 1950, Aziz Shihab, a young Palestinian journalist, arrived by boat in New York. From his passport photo, we can picture him: his dark, wavy hair, round glasses over his deep brown eyes, wearing a suit and jacket. He had received a scholarship to attend university in Kansas, where he would soon begin an extended career in writing. On the surface, he was very much an immigrant. But he was also a refugee, expelled with his family from their home just outside the walls of the Old City of Jerusalem in 1948 – his family fleeing to a village in what is today the West Bank. The loss of his home haunted Aziz for the rest of his life. So would the tension of being both immigrant and refugee; of seeking out a new life and longing for a lost one. As the boat approached New York Harbor, Aziz Shihab threw his suitcase overboard; it was never clear exactly why.

In Arabic, his last name means "shooting

Stephanie Saldaña is a writer based in the Middle East and the author of, most recently, A Country Between *(Sourcebooks, 2017). She lives in Jerusalem with her husband and children.*

"It was just that sense of no gravity," Naomi tells me when I interview her about his arrival. "What is a mailbox? What is a trashcan?"

2/

If I am writing about Aziz Shihab now, more than seventy years after his arrival in New York, it is because, in a way I'm still not sure I understand, he became a friend. I never met him. Still, he followed me, as I followed him.

From New York, Aziz traveled to Kansas, where he enrolled in university. Years later, the owner of a drugstore soda fountain there would tell Naomi that her father, a regular, always looked preoccupied sitting at the counter. "Well yes," she would write in her book *19 Varieties of Gazelle*: "That's what immigrants look like. They always have other worlds on their minds."

From her poems, from his writings, and from Naomi herself, I try to piece together some details of what Aziz's "other world" had once been. Born in Jerusalem, Aziz Shihab grew up in the Nabi Daoud quarter just outside the Old City walls. I know the house, near the tomb of King David, built of stone with arched windows overlooking the road to Bethlehem. At the time, Jerusalem remained under British control. Aziz attended the Rashidiya school for boys, near Damascus Gate on the opposite side of the Old City; every morning he crossed the Old City, alleys and spices and archways working their way into his breath, becoming part of his being. He loved the multicultural fabric of Jerusalem. A Muslim, he watched Christian pilgrims walk to Bethlehem, his father allowing him once to join, insisting he wear his best suit. He played with his Jewish neighbors. He taught himself English, becoming so fluent that he was eventually hired by the BBC to read reports on the radio.

Then, just as quickly, his entire world was gone. Or taken. The details are unclear: how he

and his family were forced from their home at gunpoint in 1948 during what Palestinians call the Nakba, or "Disaster," and Israel refers to as the War of Independence; how they "escaped with the clothes on our backs and our house keys." Aziz found his way to a part of Jerusalem under Jordanian control, renting a room in the Old City and working as a journalist. He climbed the walls of the ancient city, where he had a view of the home he'd lost.

His friend was killed beside him, a subject he never wanted to speak about. "He would completely shut down, and our mother told us never to ask him about that," Naomi tells me. "I always felt his homesickness."

Later, when he moved to Kansas, Aziz learned that many Americans misunderstood his lost homeland, as well as his Muslim faith.

Aziz Shihab, passport photo, *above*, ca. 1950; with his daughter Naomi, *below*, 1960

He introduced himself as a refugee from Jerusalem. He was going to return one day. That was how he spoke of himself when he met Miriam Allwardt, who would become his wife.

3/

Naomi Shihab Nye was born in 1952 in St. Louis. She remembers her father telling her, on a Mississippi River boat trip: *You know, I did something once from a boat. I threw my suitcase.*

"I never liked that story when I was a child," Naomi tells me. "How could you throw your stuff away? And what else was in the suitcase? Why did you do that?"

Even then, she knew there was something different about her father. He asked lots of questions. He told stories – every night, if he wasn't at work late, he would tell her stories by her bedside.

When she was fourteen, they moved to Jerusalem for a year; she walked her father's streets until they became part of her being, an experience that would find its way into her poems and novels for decades. But they didn't stay. When Naomi was seventeen, her family moved to San Antonio. Now, she, like her father, was also between worlds.

In her poem "Museum" she tells of her arrival in San Antonio, where she read about the McNay

Childhood photo of Steven Saldaña, the author's father

Art Museum, located inside an old mansion. She and her friend Sally decide to go see the famous paintings. They arrive, wandering from room to room, admiring the art, until someone behind her asks: "Where do you think you are?"

They are not in a museum at all, but in someone's house.

For years, she didn't tell anyone. Mailboxes. Trashcans. Museums. All of us, every now and then, losing the ground beneath our feet.

4/

My father, Steven Saldaña, was born in San Antonio in 1950, around the time Aziz arrived in New York. His family had lived in the city for generations, and for as long as I can remember, San Antonio was described in our household simply as *home* – the place where my father knew each street, and could recognize cardinals landing on branches, and called everyone by name. Still, much remained unspoken in our family, beginning with the ñ we never put in our last name, the Spanish of my grandparents that my father did not speak. As a child, he dressed up as Superman, the ultimate outsider, a refugee from Krypton, concealing one identity and living another.

When my parents married, they migrated north to Kansas, where I was born. Soon, we moved on to Missouri, where my father worked at a local Sears Roebuck, and took us sometimes to St. Louis to ride the boat on the Mississippi River.

When I was ten, my grandmother, sick with cancer, called us back to San Antonio. So we returned "home." My father pointed to butterflies. Bluebonnets in season.

He whispered at my bedside: "Fly. Fly far, far away."

5/

I was perhaps fifteen years old the first time I met Naomi Shihab Nye. In San Antonio, she was always referred to simply as "our poet," for she was so rooted in the city – speaking in schools, teaching children – that we could not imagine she had ever lived elsewhere. That year, I attended a poetry reading at the University of Texas in San Antonio. The poet that night was W. S. Merwin, the great translator of the natural world. I had met Merwin the year before; he came to speak to me while I was sitting beneath a tree. He was, surreally, wearing a necklace of moss around his neck, and had just finished reading at the San Antonio Book Fair. We remained in touch. Now he had returned.

The reading ended. I walked beside Merwin through the campus. Naomi Shihab Nye, long his friend, was on his other side.

"Weren't you afraid to speak in front of all of those people?" I asked Merwin.

He turned to me, his blue eyes meeting mine, and said: "Stephanie, you must never be afraid of anything."

6/

Years passed. I heeded my father's whispers, and moved far, far away, arriving in Damascus to study Arabic. I crossed the Old City streets until they became part of my being. I learned what it is to love a place that is misunderstood. When I returned home to Texas, I always carried the same gift: the famous Syrian chocolates created by the Ghraoui/Ghraowi family, known in the Middle East as among the finest chocolatiers in the world. I relished the ritual of visiting the store in Damascus, where the staff patiently waited on me as I chose every piece of handcrafted chocolate, carefully wrapped, each more delicate than the last.

By the time I arrived in Texas, I felt too tired to explain: *In Damascus, light falls on stone. The people are kind. They'll invite any stranger to coffee. They're musicians. Artisans. I've never met people who pay such attention to beauty.*

So instead, I opened the box of chocolates. *Here. Taste this.*

7/

In Syria I fell in love with a man from France, and we married. In 2006, we moved to Jerusalem. The following year, Aziz Shihab died. "Are you home now?" Naomi asks him at the opening of her book of poems, *Transfer.*

My father, by then president of Catholic Charities in San Antonio, began helping to resettle refugees from all over the world. Maybe it was that memory of Superman. Maybe he hoped that someone was taking care of me, too, on the other side of the world. Maybe there was a side of my father I'd never imagined. He worked tirelessly, and men and women from Sudan and Iraq and Afghanistan and Iran settled in our streets. *They'll feel at home here,* my father explained to me. Knowing that Naomi's father had also been a refugee, my father reached out to her, asking her to help him at charity events.

So they became friends, and my father was soon convinced that Naomi could somehow connect him to me, bridging the distance between us. In 2008, he gave me two books for Christmas. The first was Naomi's book of poems about the Middle East: *19 Varieties of Gazelle*; inside, my father handwrote me a letter: *Stephanie: Thank you for opening the world to me . . .*

The other volume was Aziz Shihab's cookbook of recipes and memories.

I settled into my home in Jerusalem to read. That is how I learned that I was living in the neighborhood where Aziz Shihab had walked every day as a boy before his exile. His school stood around the corner from my home.

So I began to walk in his footsteps. Past the school. Through the market. In front of the Church of Gethsemane, where he had played with friends. *I remember you. I remember you.*

8/

My father died in 2012 after a terrible battle with cancer. At home for the funeral, I found his copy of Aziz Shihab's memoir: *Does the Land Remember Me?*

Naomi had written inside: "To Steve. From the daughter of Aziz." I carried it back with me to Jerusalem.

I visited home only once after that. Naomi met me in a coffee shop, and we spoke of our fathers. Two grieving daughters. A sense of no gravity.

By then Syria had erupted into civil war. The United States closed its doors to almost all refugees. I traveled the world, seeking fragments, as Syrians scattered across the globe. In Paris, a man from Aleppo still making soap. In Amman, Syrians pounding pistachio ice cream.

I searched for the chocolate. I discovered that the branch of the family that spelled their name *Ghraoui* had opened a chocolate shop in Budapest. Their cousins, who spelled it *Ghraowi,* opened a store in Corpus Christi, Texas. This seemed impossible.

I couldn't bring myself to visit. It would make the war real. In any case, before long, the chocolate shop in Texas closed, as though only a dream.

9/

I traveled to Iraq. At a table, Syrians in exile shared what they missed about home. The apricots. Pomegranates. *Ghraowi chocolates,* I suggested.

The man beside me sighed. "You win," he said.

10/

In 2020 everyone seemed to be reading Naomi Shihab Nye's poetry. Friends, exiled in their homes because of Covid-19, forwarded her poem "Gate A–4," about an old Palestinian woman losing her bearings in an airport terminal when her flight is delayed. Naomi meets her, speaks to her in halting Arabic, and watches as the scene is transformed: They call the woman's son to give him news, then Naomi's father to speak in Arabic, then friends. Soon, the woman hands out *ma'amoul* cookies, dusted with sugar, to exhausted passengers. "And I looked around that gate of late and weary ones and thought, This is the world I want to live in," Naomi writes.

When Naomi received a lifetime achievement award from the National Book Critics Circle, I wrote from Jerusalem to congratulate her. In a surreal twist, the award was presented to her by Michael Schaub, my childhood best friend, who had grown up to become a book critic.

In her reply she mentioned, almost as an afterthought, that she had just lent my book about Syria to a beloved student of hers in Texas. "She's from Damascus," she wrote. "Her name is Nour Al Ghraowi. Her father owns a chocolate factory."

11/

Nour Al Ghraowi grew up in Damascus, near the base of Mount Qasioun. Beneath her house stood a chocolate factory, where her father, Bashar Ghraowi, fashioned some of the finest chocolate in the Middle East. She awakened in the morning to the smell of chocolate wafting through the windows. When she descended to the factory, she saw her father and his assistants crafting chocolate by hand: mixing butter and milk and sugar and cocoa, pouring chocolate into molds, placing each pistachio. Her grandfather, Tayseer Ghraowi, had been one of the first Syrians to bring chocolate to the country. Even today, her father kept the recipes a secret.

"I used to tell him: You need to tell me the secrets," Nour told me when I interviewed her. "I don't want to work in chocolate. But still, I want the secrets."

For Nour, the factory became a school for mastering the art of the particular. Her father molded chocolates into pyramids or flat disks or flowers. Each was wrapped individually in special paper: "My dad loves colors," Nour explains. "You'll find orange, purple, yellow, silver, gold. The stickers could be flowers, triangles, squares. They all had my father's name on them."

He worked in the factory in the mornings, pausing with the family for lunch. In the afternoons, Nour often accompanied him to

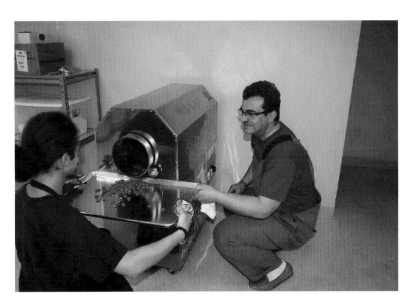

Nour Al Ghraowi with her father, 2016

the chocolate store in the center of the city. Customers came in, asking for chocolate-dipped cherries, apricots, and dates; chocolate-covered coffee beans; or *raha,* a sweet filled with pistachios and rolled in rose petals.

Nour watched. All of this became part of her. In the meantime, she taught herself to speak English, and scribbled poems in notebooks. She began to study literature at Damascus University.

Now she wonders if those days with her father found their way into her poems.

"A five-line poem can tell an entire story," she explains. But only if you pay attention to every line break. Every word. Every sound.

12/

In 2011, war broke out in Syria. Nour applied for a visa to the United States. She was denied three times. Her family traveled to Egypt. She begged her father to return to Damascus so she could finish her studies.

So she and her father did. In her poem, "Melting Candles," Nour describes studying by candlelight, racing against the melting wax, trying to finish her books. Bombs exploding outside.

She applied for a visa one last time. It worked. She arrived in Austin, Texas, on December 31, 2013.

None of her studies transferred. She started over from scratch, enrolling at the local community college. Her parents and brother arrived in Texas three years later, with a business visa to open a chocolate shop in nearby Corpus Christi. They purchased the machines. They began to make chocolates. Newspapers ran stories about a famous Syrian chocolate family, starting over in Texas. But her parents couldn't speak English. When Nour had to translate for her father, she saw how hard that was for him to bear.

Before long, her parents and brother returned to Damascus. They would continue making chocolates there, despite the war.

Nour remained in the United States, transferring to the University of Texas at Austin, where she picked up a minor in creative writing. She didn't see herself as a refugee. She didn't see herself as an immigrant either. When she introduced herself, she said: "I'm from Syria."

She fell in love with writing poems. "I felt that I had that power," she tells me, "that power of a poem that can tell a lot. Especially that I had a lot to tell."

As she prepared to graduate, a professor told her about a Palestinian-American poet named Naomi Shihab Nye, who taught in the MFA program at Texas State University.

He suggested that she go to meet her. As if to say: *With her, you might feel at home.*

Nour began to read Naomi Shihab Nye's poems. She saw that she sometimes even used Arabic in her verses. She wrote about familiar olive trees.

Nour made the long drive to San Marcos. On the first day of class, she turned to Naomi Shihab Nye and said to her: "You're the reason I'm here."

Now, I settle in my room in Jerusalem and open Nour Al Ghraowi's not-yet-published book of poems. I'm drawn in, again, to the Damascus streets I haven't walked in fifteen years. Jasmine and war, a life lived between languages, the Barada River. Among the fragments: her father, fashioning chocolate. Her father, kissing her goodnight. Her father, buying candles so that she might study against the dark.

13/

We remember each other into being. We find one another across the distance.

At the end of Naomi Shihab Nye's poem, "My Father and the Fig Tree," Aziz Shihab finally discovers his fig tree in Texas. Or perhaps it finds him. Later, he plants a branch in Naomi's backyard, so that she will have one too.

Today, she sits beside it nearly every day, talking to him across the void. ➤

Eyvind Earle,
Pine Branch,
gouache, 1955

Wreathmaking

The hard, dark berries, blue as black
snakes are blue, befogged with newness, clench
their pips in scaly tufts of green, each branch
an elenchus of logic, a spray of craze, an attack

on soft fingers walking through them, your
fingers calling shape from the bedlam of life
with brutal twists of form. You flick the knife
to smooth a stem, a cedar stem; its fur

heaps greenly on your shoes, as if you'd skinned
a wooly tree, not trimmed it, to make a wreath.
Completed circle, made of endings, shaped

to hint what never ends, it tricks and bends
the eye to green forevers, clever deaths
of death, where girls and berries do escape.

FORESTER MCCLATCHEY

The End

A Black Panther in prison makes a reckoning.

# of Rage

Ashley Lucas

The Story of Russell
Maroon Shoatz

Father, Panther, Soldier, Spy

In 2014 in Pennsylvania, Russell Maroon Shoatz was released from twenty-two consecutive years of solitary confinement into the general prison population. This is twenty-one years and fifty weeks longer than the length of time in solitary the United Nations has deemed to be torture. Having spent so much time in a small space, he had trouble walking and could not climb the stairs to the cafeteria. He felt overwhelmed by other people, whose presence he had so desperately missed for all those years. Known to his supporters inside and outside the prison as a Black liberation leader, he now found it physically difficult to stand up tall. That he was even alive was more than many who considered him a cop killer wanted: they believed that his punishment should have been death.

Later that same year, in Ferguson, Missouri, Michael Brown was fatally shot by police officer Darren Wilson. Brown's body was left in the street for several hours and no charges were ever filed against the officer. In response, Black Lives Matter bloomed into a protest movement. Despite all that had changed since Russell went to prison in 1972, this was a direct echo of the past. Nearly fifty years before, in Philadelphia, he had witnessed a similar killing of a young Black man by a police officer, even down to

the body neglected by authorities on the scene and the lack of repercussions. This and other such events catalyzed Russell and his activist friends to become militant revolutionaries.

Not long before, in 1966, another Black leader had warned that people were losing faith in the democratic process and nonviolent change. "Those who make this peaceful revolution impossible will make a violent revolution inevitable," said Martin Luther King Jr., standard-bearer for the peaceful revolution, with a message directed at those in power. Of course, the powerful did not want even a nonviolent revolution, and instead cracked down on dissidents of all stripes.

In Philadelphia, where Russell lived, Frank Rizzo became police commissioner in 1967 and was later elected mayor. As the number of Black people shot or killed by police spiked under his leadership, Rizzo made it known that no allegations of police misconduct would be investigated under his watch. The killings and lack of accountability inspired an abundance of activism that ranged from the formation of civic organizations focused on registering the city's Black voters to a variety of militant Black nationalist groups. In turn, Rizzo formed a Civil Defense Squad to aggressively gather information on left-wing activists (including students), alternative-newspaper publishers, and Black revolutionaries. The FBI modeled its COINTELPRO surveillance program on Rizzo's Civil Defense Squad and used it to launch a national campaign to harass and disrupt leftist radicals, including the Black Panther Party.

Russell was among these radicals, living underground as a member of Philadelphia's Black Liberation Army, a highly secretive revolutionary group connected to but distinct from the Black Panthers. In 1972, he was arrested and convicted of the politically motivated August 29, 1970, shooting of two White police officers, Sergeant Frank Von Colln (who died) and Patrolman James Harrington (who lived). Russell later escaped from prison twice.

To some in the Philadelphia radical community of the early 1970s, Russell was a freedom fighter, taking up arms against the true sources of terror in the United States: the authorities who dealt violence to

Ashley Lucas teaches theatre at the University of Michigan, where she works with the Prison Creative Arts Project and the Carceral State Project. She is the author of Prison Theatre and the Global Crisis of Incarceration *(Methuen Drama, 2020).*

Blacks and other minorities. To these authorities, he was a dangerous political extremist. To his family, he was an absence – the father who wasn't there. To the families of two police officers, he was the source of terrible grief.

Russell became many other versions of himself in the decades that followed. His conception of his own identity, beliefs, and political philosophies transformed and contradicted themselves over and over again. His story, emblematic as it is of an era when young people went to one extreme after another to transform an unjust world, has never been told at this length before. It tells us much about racism, violence, suffering, public safety, law enforcement, and social transformation. The most important thing it tells us is that no true story, however detailed, can make all these forms of suffering balance out against each other, as in a ledger. An honest account can only push us up against their complexities, again and again.

The year Russell went to prison, his son and namesake Russell III went to kindergarten. In a profound sense, they were each on their own at the beginning of something momentous – one having just received a life sentence and the other starting school without a father, neither one of them with any way to reach out to the other. Russell III would not comprehend the events that led to his father's incarceration or the context surrounding them for many years, and had no idea that it would become his life's work to advocate for his father's release. Something else happened at the same time that would also change the course of Russell III's life – his informal adoption by a police officer, who could easily have been the one shot that night.

Born in 1941 in North Carolina, Claude Barnes knew the terrors of the segregated South and felt keenly his powerlessness to combat them. From childhood, he dreamed of becoming a police officer – someone who could hold authority and help end the violence that threatened everyday people. He says that in his youth his motives were not always pure. He was envious of those with power and wanted some of his own. By the time he reached his mid-twenties, Barnes had become a devout Christian and believed that he could serve God and his people by joining the Philadelphia police force, which he did in November 1966. He married and started a family. His son Reggie

wound up in the same kindergarten class as a boy who seemed to need a friend.

Claude Barnes loved being a father and was eager to embrace and mentor all the boys in the neighborhood, especially those who befriended Reggie. When Barnes met Russell III, he unknowingly stood at a crucial intersection of two powerful forces in the child's life: fathering and policing. Barnes was on the Philadelphia police force in August 1970 when six officers were shot in three different incidents on

Frank Rizzo, Philadelphia's police commissioner (1968-71) and mayor (1972-80)

Claude "Papa" Barnes, a Philadelphia police officer (retired) and bishop of the Church of Faith on North 38th Street

the same weekend. The historical record suggests that none of the individual policemen had been specifically targeted. The assailants had been willing to shoot any officer they encountered, rather than seeking out particular policemen who had records of racist or brutal behavior. If Barnes had been on duty on August 29, he could have been one of the men Russell Shoatz and others were later convicted of shooting. Barnes had, of course, heard about these cases, but he did not immediately make the connection to the kindergartener who spent many afternoons at his home. In time, the boy would say things about his father that made Barnes understand who he was. "Quite naturally, that gave me mixed emotions because I loved Russell, and I also knew that his father was a very important part of his life," Barnes says. Russell III knew that the man he came to

63

call Papa Barnes worked as a police officer, but the significance of that fact did not register for him just yet.

As a Black officer who worked for years under Frank Rizzo, Barnes knew all too well the tensions between trying to keep communities safe and the racist and deadly potential of policing. Barnes did his best to keep people safe and to be a role model for the youth in his community. He managed this remarkably well, never once pointing his service revolver at anyone in the twenty years he was on the force. For ten of those years, Barnes worked as part of a community-relations police unit, "trying to educate the people on how they could resolve problems in their own neighborhood without calling the police."

Growing up six blocks away from where his father had lived as a child, Russell III describes the "frightening times" brought on his neighborhood by Rizzo's police force. He routinely watched Black men

Malcolm X, 1964: "We are nonviolent with people who are nonviolent with us."

"just getting it" from the cops. An institution meant to keep the peace, protect the people, and "stop injustice from happening" has not played anything like this role in his life or that of his peers. It takes "constant ducking and dodging just to be a human" and a police officer at the same time, Russell III says. He calls this the "cop dance" and admires Papa Barnes for having the strength to do it for decades.

Russell III and Papa Barnes became so attached to one another that they consider themselves family and requested that I interview them together for this story. Barnes's own father was distant, and he says he recognized himself in Russell III and understood how it felt to have a father who existed but was not there when you needed him. When I asked Barnes if his colleagues on the force knew that he had a close relationship with the son of a man convicted of

killing a fellow officer, he said he had never thought to tell anyone at work: Russell III is like his own son, and that's no one else's business. At this point in our conversation, Russell III thanked Papa Barnes and said he had not previously been brave enough to state publicly that "my non-biological father is a police officer." Barnes replied, "You have nothing to be ashamed of."

His love for Russell III and his understanding that sometimes "the system works against African Americans" make Barnes wish that he could speak to the elder Russell. Barnes would like to ask Russell what he was thinking on the night of the crime that sent him to prison and give him a police officer's perspective on it. Barnes also would like to tell Russell more about his son, what he has been doing all these years, and what a good man Russell III grew up to be. Most of all, Barnes wants Russell to know that he can still make the best of however much time he has left on this earth. Barnes says, "It's not how you start off. It's how you finish." He wants Russell to offer up a sincere, public apology to those he has harmed and to find peace before the end of his life. Barnes is praying for God to touch Russell's heart, for God to lead Russell toward reconciliation and redemption.

Until now, Russell has never offered such an apology.

The Making of a Revolutionary

Russell Shoatz still remembers the first time he saw racist violence. As a small child in the 1940s, he watched as two White police officers responded to a call about domestic violence in a working-class Black area of Philadelphia. The neighbors watched from their porches and windows as the policemen dragged a man from his house, beating him and hurling racial epithets as they shoved him into the car. One of the policemen turned to the onlookers and asked, "Any of you other n----rs want any of this?"

From his preteen years onward, Russell had ugly interactions with law enforcement. By the time he was thirteen, he and his friends had come to accept police brutality as a routine part of their lives. They were regularly roughed up by patrolmen and told to expect this by the "old heads" – the more grown-up gang members in their neighborhood. Russell describes a culture of frequent brawls between opposing gangs, and old heads coercing adolescent boys to become drug runners. Also, the old heads' dismissive and sometimes brutal treatment of women influenced his own behavior toward women in his life.

Russell spent several stints in juvenile detention facilities, including a wilderness camp for wayward youth where he learned survival skills that he would later employ after an escape from adult prison. By his teenage years in the late 1950s he was a self-described "street thug."

The moment that changed Russell's life took place on a New York street corner in 1963, where he saw Malcolm X address a rally. "Within the first five minutes of hearing Malcolm speak, I knew this was not a man like any that I knew or ever heard about." Malcolm's descriptions of "police brutality, the brutality that the community members visited on each other, [and] the absurdity of demanding that civil rights demonstrators not defend themselves from attack" gave Russell a new framework for understanding his own life. Russell saw in Malcolm a figure of strength with a more noble purpose than the old heads on the corner. He committed himself to turning his life in this direction but did not know where to begin.

It wasn't until after Malcolm X's assassination a few years later that Russell found his way to the Muntu Cultural Center, a community space run by a Philadelphia organization called the Black Coalition. There, he learned to take pride in his African heritage instead of feeling shame; he immersed himself in art, music, food, stories, and traditions. He was inspired by the group's leaders, who called on the Black community to come together and stand up for itself.

Building on their encounters with local activists, Russell, his sister Gloria, and several others decided to form their own group called the Black Unity Council. The BUC's original intent was to start another community center with a food bank, daycare, gang intervention programs, and a "liberation school" to educate Black children about their history. The BUC successfully organized a Black caucus within a local union to protect the interests of workers ignored by the White leadership, and won significant gains for its members.

Interacting with the BUC was also the first step toward changing Russell's view of women. As part of the community's accountability, the men "could be hauled before the group and judged because of any of their former practices that brutalized women. In turn, this gave the women more freedom to speak their minds." He came to see "that women could and would exhibit courage in situations that made most men withdraw in fear." Meanwhile, he worked on deconstructing other behaviors from his old gang life, trying to defuse what he now saw as pointless scrapping among the young boys of the neighborhood. In talking them out of a planned violent retaliation against another gang, "I was not able to offer them anything in return for not doing this except to constantly repeat the idea that we should not be killing each other over much of nothing."

Russell had always been skeptical of nonviolent resistance in the civil rights movement. "I had been

By the time he was thirteen, Russell and his friends had come to accept police brutality as a routine part of their lives.

taught that one did not allow another to attack them, under any circumstances!" Though he developed a grudging respect for the courage peaceful demonstrators showed under duress, when he became politically engaged he was convinced that their actions could not deliver Black people from oppression.

Sometime in the late 1960s, Russell witnessed a particularly harrowing police killing of a young Black man in his neighborhood. Officers on Rizzo's force engaged in a car chase with a man suspected of joyriding. When the young man abandoned the car and ran away on foot, an officer pursued him to his home and shot him as he tried to hide behind his mother. The son managed to run into the yard, where the officer shot him several more times. The mother grabbed a kitchen knife and stabbed the cop to try to defend her son. As her son's body lay on the ground, a crowd of neighbors, including Russell, were drawn to the yard. The paramedics who arrived left the son's body lying and set about treating the officer. The mother stood over her son in a pool of blood and told everyone gathered what had happened. Before this moment, Russell had always accepted whatever violence the police had meted out to him and his friends. As he listened to this mother, something in him shifted: "I almost lost control of myself and had to fight down an urge to jump one of the policemen that was mingling in the

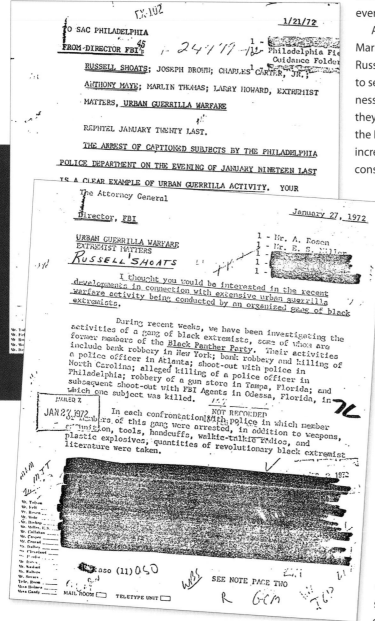

COINTELPRO files on Russell Shoatz show the direct involvement of J. Edgar Hoover, director of the FBI, and John N. Mitchell, the US attorney general, who would himself be imprisoned as a conspirator in the Watergate scandal.

crowd . . . to take his weapon and shoot him with it." He refrained from retaliating that day but resolved to take a new kind of action: community organizing to prevent further police murders.

To address this killing, various groups, including the BUC, convened a series of forums, some of which included police representatives. It quickly became clear to the activists that the authorities had no intention of offering a meaningful response. In a meeting with the slain boy's mother, Russell learned that her report of the event had been administratively buried, as if none of it had ever happened.

After the assassination of Martin Luther King Jr. in 1968, Russell and several others set fire to several White-owned businesses in their neighborhood that they believed were exploiting the Black residents. Becoming increasingly radicalized and considering nonviolent strategies to be dead ends, they decided that the BUC needed a paramilitary wing. Russell and his comrades "believed that militia-style organizations that were set up, organized, trained, and controlled by the Black community" could protect Black efforts at political organizing and community projects. In a 2006 interview, he said, "Rightly or wrongly, the BUC had reached the conclusion that in order for Blacks in the United States to be truly free, we would have to wage armed struggle."

This was a period of US history in which all over the country young people of various racial, ethnic, and social backgrounds were going underground – forming secretive radical groups which bombed corporate and government targets, helped their comrades escape from prisons, and killed police officers. Some of this political violence happened in protest of US military operations in Vietnam, but often it took the form of retaliatory responses to police or FBI killings of Black people. These groups thought a revolution was coming and soon. In his 2015 book *Days of Rage*, Bryan Burrough characterizes the story of the underground as "ultimately a tragic tale, defined by one unavoidable irony: that so many idealistic young Americans, passionately committed to creating a better world for themselves and those less fortunate, believed they had to kill people to do it."

Russell would become one of these young people, helping to form the Philadelphia cell of an amorphous group – one so secretive and little-documented that researchers of the period cannot even be sure that the various groups using this name knew about each other – called the Black Liberation Army.

Offense as Defense

While the Black Panthers, formed in 1966 in Oakland, California, were gaining notoriety and seeding new chapters across the country, the BUC stayed small and local with a decidedly militant mindset. By the summer of 1969, the BUC had acquired a significant amount of weaponry, even including a box of US military hand grenades, and had to keep a low profile to avoid discovery. This put a damper on the charter members' plans to establish a daycare and community center, and caused the departure of the majority of the BUC's members. After the split, only about eight men and their female partners remained in the group, including Russell and the woman who would become his common-law wife. The group decided to rename themselves the Black Liberation Army (BLA) – a moniker they adopted because they had heard of such a group in Washington, DC. At the time they had no knowledge of or connection to what would later come to be the more famous New York–based organization using that name, which included Assata Shakur and Sekou Odinga.

After the December 1969 murder of Fred Hampton (subject of the 2021 biopic *Judas and the Black Messiah*), who was drugged by an FBI informant and shot by Chicago police as he slept next to his pregnant girlfriend, Russell and his BLA comrades decided to stay close to the Panther chapter in Philadelphia to "upgrade their defenses and react to the expected attacks" from police.

Meanwhile, the national Panther organization had the same kinds of ideological differences that led to the dissolution of the BUC, egged on by interference from COINTELPRO. The assassination of a young

Panther field marshal named Robert Webb, which was blamed on a rival Panther faction but evidence suggests may have been done by COINTELPRO, was the catalyst for the creation of the New York cells of the Black Liberation Army. What is known about the activities of any of these factions can only be told in fragments. The secrecy, anger, and fear that shrouded the actions of the BLA, the Panthers, the FBI, and the police prevent even those involved in these organizations from fully knowing what occurred. In a 2006 interview, Russell described this as a necessary strategy to enable revolutionary actions:

John Clutchette, George Jackson, and Fleeta Drumgo (the "Soledad Brothers"), 1970

People must understand that in dealing with the history of the Black Panther Party, nobody – not the Panthers, not the police/FBI or other repressive arms of the state – knows it all! . . . A lot of stuff was so delicate that it was known and handled only by those who needed to know about it, the downside to this being that if things didn't go right, or if you got caught, you were on your own.

Unlike groups such as the Weather Underground, the BLA did not release substantial political manifestos describing its philosophies or its vision for the revolution. It was not a formal part of the Black Panther

Party, though the vast majority of the BLA's members had been Panthers at some point. What seemed to unite all the members of the various BLA cells was their sense that the necessary response to the ongoing police murders of young Black people was to respond in kind by killing policemen.

Gunshots

August 7, 1970: Seventeen-year-old Black Panther Jonathan Jackson and five accomplices used shotguns to take over a courtroom in the Marin County Courthouse in northern California and demand the release of a group of Panthers known as the Soledad Brothers, including Jonathan's brother George. Five

Behind every successful or failed revolution, there are the untold stories of people who keep life going day to day, picking up the pieces and caring for the children.

hostages, including the judge, prosecutor, and three jurors, left the courthouse at gunpoint. The ensuing gun battle with police left Jonathan, two other Panthers, and the judge dead. The prosecutor and another Panther suffered serious wounds. Jonathan Jackson became a martyr to the Panthers and an inspiration to Russell Shoatz. "This is what so many of us had been waiting and training for," he recounts in his unpublished 2001 autobiography. "My feeling was, in street language: the shit was on!"

August 29, 1970: Thirty-nine-year-old Patrolman James Harrington was driving with his partner, Henry Kenner, in a police van about one hundred yards away from the guard house at Fairmount Park in Philadelphia when an unknown man waved them down – Harrington assumed to ask for directions – and then, without a word, shot him point blank. The bullet entered his chin and came out the back of his neck. Harrington lived. Kenner, a Black officer, was unharmed. Blood and bone fragments filled what was left of Harrington's mouth as he tried to radio for help. His injuries cost him his teeth and lower jaw, as well as full hearing loss in one ear and partial in the other.

Half an hour later, forty-three-year-old Sergeant Frank Von Colln sat talking on the phone at his desk at the guard house. An unidentified man fatally shot

Von Colln five times. No clear evidence was ever found to identify the shooter in either case. However, in his autobiography Russell admits to being "at the immediate scene of those events" and asserts that these acts were "carried out in accord with and at the behest of the leadership of the Black Panther Party."

August 30, 1970: In two separate incidents, four more Philadelphia police officers were shot. Russell references one of these shootings as being carried out by comrades in another underground cell affiliated with his. Another source claims that these later shootings proved not to be linked to the prior day's violence or the Panthers, but police commissioner Frank Rizzo – a man not in the habit of making careful distinctions among Black people – and many others assumed that the Panthers were behind all of these attacks on police. Rizzo ordered 5 a.m. raids of Black Panther offices in three different Philadelphia neighborhoods.

Three suspects (Hugh Williams and brothers Robert and Alvin Joyner) were arrested within days, and a fourth (Fred Burton) surrendered a month later, but Russell Shoatz was not found in any of these raids. He had already gone underground, and would not be caught until January 19, 1972, when he was arrested under a false name on a weapons charge. His fingerprints revealed his identity and alerted the police that he was wanted for the Fairmount Park shootings.

These five men were ultimately convicted of the Harrington shooting and Von Colln murder. (A sixth suspect, Richard Bernard Thomas, was captured in 1996, twenty-six years after the attack, living under a new identity. He was acquitted, as witness testimony had deteriorated in the intervening years.) The victims' families wanted the defendants to receive the death penalty. Four of the men known during their trials as the Philadelphia Five are serving life without parole sentences in Pennsylvania prisons for first-degree murder. (Life sentences in Pennsylvania exclude the possibility of parole.) Russell, who was portrayed as the ringleader and later received extra sentences for two successful prison breaks, is serving two life sentences plus twenty-five years. All of the Philadelphia Five were offered sentence reductions if they would give evidence against the others, but none did so. They made a pact to one another that half a century of incarceration has not eroded.

The Revolutionary's Family

For most of the three years before the FBI came to her house looking for him, Thelma Christian had no idea where her husband had gone. Moreover, she didn't care.

To those FBI agents, on that day in late 1970 or early 1971, Russell was a terrorist. To Thelma, he was merely a difficult and absent husband. It was no simple matter for a twenty-six-year-old Black woman in Philadelphia to support herself and her four young children, but Thelma was relieved not to have to deal with the abuse that had ended when her husband left.

Thelma hadn't seen Russell in months when he appeared on her doorstep earlier on the same day she received a visit from the FBI. He was sweaty and looked like he had been running. Thelma let him into the house but only for a moment. Russell wanted to see his children, but Thelma told him they were staying with her family in Virginia for the summer. She thought there was something strange going on but didn't want to question him. He left within minutes, and she was glad to see him go.

Then without warning the FBI arrived with guns and pushed their way into her house. Thelma was terrified. They came in asking for Russell, and she told them he had just left. When the door closed behind them, she almost passed out. This incident was the first indication she had that her husband was wanted by the police or that he might have committed a serious crime.

For years to come, Thelma would assume her phone was tapped. She thought she could hear the sound of a machine recording her, so she seldom made calls. She would be questioned on multiple occasions and given a lie detector test, which she failed because she was so nervous. Though every authority with whom she came into contact ultimately concluded that Thelma knew nothing of Russell's revolutionary activities, her home would be raided multiple times – the doors kicked in, SWAT teams pulling things off the walls, helicopters circling overhead, men with guns surrounding her house and endangering her and her children.

Thelma had separated from her husband three years prior to the crimes for which he would be convicted. Despite this, for the last fifty years, her life and the lives of her children have been profoundly shaped by violence and surveillance at the hands of law enforcement agents, the courts that gave them warrants, and the public's judgment of actions of which she had no knowledge and in which she did not participate.

Behind every successful or failed revolution, there are the untold stories of people who keep life going day to day, picking up the pieces and caring for the children. In the Shoatz family, this fell to Thelma.

When Thelma Married Russell

Thelma says she never liked the man who would become her husband. She had moved to Philadelphia from Virginia with two of her older sisters and was starting a new life in the big city. From the moment Russell met her he pursued her aggressively, although she refused him many times. It was the early 1960s, and many men still lived a script that portrayed such persistence as romantic. Thelma eventually relented and went out with him. They found out a few weeks later that she was pregnant.

The Shoatz family insisted on a wedding and paid for everything. No one asked Thelma what she wanted or how she felt about it. When she and Russell married in March of 1964, she cried throughout the ceremony. Later that year she gave birth to their daughter Theresa. When the two new parents went to the doctor for her postpartum checkup, they discovered that another baby (their daughter Sharon) was already on the way. They would have four children in as many years.

Thelma had her own political interests; she was involved in the civil rights movement, including the march across the Edmund Pettus Bridge in Selma, Alabama, where John Lewis was clubbed by state troopers and she sustained injuries herself. Still, she remained committed to the cause of nonviolent demonstration. With so many young children, she was mostly tied to the home front anyway. Her life was no longer her own.

Thelma and Russell's marriage deteriorated quickly, accelerated by his philandering and aggression. He was struggling to reconcile the life he had known with Malcolm X's vision of the revolution, wanting change but not knowing how. During this period, Russell met a woman nicknamed Bonnie (legal name Loretta Fairly), who was also married with children but separated from her husband. The two bonded over their similarly chaotic lives as they became both lovers and friends. Though Russell wanted to stay married to Thelma, he turned to Bonnie for emotional intimacy and comfort.

He got into fights with men in the neighborhood and hit Thelma when they argued. On one such occasion, she ran out of the house and called the police. Russell shut the door when the police asked to come into his home, and though they could see clearly through the front window that he was unarmed and wearing only his underwear, they broke down the door, beat him into submission, and hauled him to the station.

When Russell's father bailed him out of jail the next day, he told his son he should have used his shotgun on the officers when they broke down his door. This was uncharacteristic for Russell Sr., who until then had tried to teach his son to keep his head down and play by the rules. Russell describes his parents as "under the illusion that if they just helped me become a healthy, educated member of the broader society, from that start I had an excellent chance of becoming a stable and productive member of the community. Many years later I would hear them both say that their visions were doomed because of forces they never imagined would come into play, though being from the segregated and repressive Southern states, they were aware of them. They just thought they had escaped them."

In 1967 Russell was present at the hospital for Thelma's delivery of their son Russell III. Less than a year later, Thelma gave birth to their last baby, a girl named Tammy, but by this point, the couple had split. Russell became more committed to Bonnie, and around the time Tammy was born, Bonnie became pregnant with the first of the three children she would have with Russell – Hassan, Naeemah, and Jalilah. This period coincided with Russell's awakening to Black liberation, a cause in which Bonnie was also engaged.

Meanwhile, Thelma took her four young children back to Virginia. After struggling to care for them,

Thelma agreed to let the two oldest, Theresa and Sharon, return to Philadelphia to live with their father and Bonnie for a while. In the two years that Russell and Bonnie were raising Thelma's girls, they had a large blackboard, a desk, and chairs set up in the living room. They wanted the children to have a "revolutionary education." Russell "had hopes of preparing them to carry on our Liberation Struggle, as I felt sure I would either be killed or jailed."

After two years, Thelma returned to reclaim her daughters, and she was appalled at the state in which she found them. Thelma would never leave any of her children in Russell's care again, despite her profound struggles to support them on her own. Neither Russell's family nor her own helped Thelma stay afloat financially or took them in when they needed a place to live. She soon found herself homeless. Theresa remembers walking with her mother and siblings, knocking on doors to ask for a place to stay. The Great Migration was still bringing southerners north to Philadelphia to look for work, and the answer they got at every door was, "We already took in a lot of people." At last the family came to a house owned by a man called Mr. Ben, who initially told them, "We're filled. We got a house full of people just like you." When Thelma told her story, Mr. Ben found a place for them on the enclosed back porch. Theresa remembers being desperately cold sleeping there, but during their first night other people Mr. Ben had taken in gave Thelma and her children some of the few blankets they had.

Thelma was immensely grateful for the kindness of these strangers but still often found it nearly impossible to go on. She would cry out, "Where are you, God, where are you? Do you see all of this stuff I'm going through? Where are you?" When she was on the edge of despair, she would look at her babies and remember that they had no one but her, and she would resolve again to trust in God. "He is my provider, my protector, and I can go to him for anything that I need."

The Fog of War

During this period, Russell, Bonnie, and their children were having adventures of a very different kind, arming themselves and engaging in combat training. Bonnie was a better marksman than any of the men in the BUC. She and Russell had many weapons stored in their home and practiced putting their children in a cast-iron bathtub to protect them in the event of a shootout with the police.

Russell's account of this time describes a harrowing near-miss for one of his children. One night, Bonnie was helping one of their comrades make his way to a safe house through streets full of police officers. This man and Bonnie decided they could get through walking casually if Bonnie carried her infant daughter in her arms. Russell's autobiography explains, "Their plan in case of an emergency was for her to throw the baby on a lawn and for him to hold her as a hostage/shield. It might sound crazy now, but that was the frame of mind that we were all in."

I wrote him about this episode, wanting to know where a revolutionary draws the line between making a better world for his family and future generations and protecting that family long enough for the children to have a future. I hoped he would tell me what he was thinking that night or in those years. Instead, he replied:

> It took me until I was in my seventies to realize just how dominated my life has been by RAGE, HUMILI-ATION, and for most of that time TESTOSTERONE. YOUTH also played a part until I was able to spend a lot of time reading, and thus being able to better understand life. There is NO way that I can express how DOMINANT RAGE has been most of my life! So much so until it made me very INSENSITIVE to others' feelings or welfare; including my loved ones and offspring. The RAGE was fed by a deep sense of HUMILIATION.

This struck me as the most honest thing he could have said about not only himself but a period of revolutionary culture that so many have struggled to understand. Russell and Bonnie as a young couple seem not only to have been driven by a revolutionary spirit, fueled by rage and humiliation, but also caught in "the fog of war"—a phrase made famous by former Secretary of Defense Robert McNamara to describe impaired decision-making during conflict. When all you see is the war, what the enemy does and what you must do in response, the context falls away, even the things for which you thought you were fighting.

After the shooting in 1970, Russell spent two years underground, traveling incognito through various states and building relationships with fellow travelers, including a group of radical nuns. Bonnie fled with him at first but eventually went back to Philadelphia to care for their children. Meanwhile he was recruiting revolutionaries, raising support, and making connections to like-minded movements around the world.

When all you see is the war, what the enemy does and what you must do in response, the context falls away, even the things for which you thought you were fighting.

In 1972, back in Philadelphia, police following up on a burglary stopped him on the street and found him carrying a large number of weapons. He was then identified as wanted for the 1970 shootings. Facing a new chapter in prison, he steeled his resolve. Looking back on this time, he wrote in 2001:

> The martyred Black Panther Fred Hampton once said, to be a revolutionary is to be an enemy of the state. To be arrested for this struggle is to be a political prisoner. I had become a political prisoner of this war that our oppressors had been waging against people of African descent, ever since kidnapping our ancestors from our mother continent of Africa. We had fought back, using every means at our disposal and to the best of our ability; and I had no regrets associated with my action. So, although my situation looked extremely critical and bleak to some, I was determined to remain faithful to the things I had been fighting for, come what may.

Forty-Nine Years in Prison

There was no question that Russell would try to escape from prison. He was a freedom fighter, after all. Insisting on a distinction between acts of war and the charges for which he was convicted and imprisoned, he viewed himself not as a criminal but as a political prisoner like the imprisoned militants of Nelson Mandela's African National Congress in apartheid South Africa: "Our resistance, insurrection, and rebellion was seditious, in as much as it was acts of war against an oppressive and unjust authority," his autobiography explains. Without acknowledging specifically what those acts might have been, Russell rejected the meaning assigned them by the court. He was a soldier in a war against the police, a war he did not start, and held that his activities should be interpreted within that context.

Apparently, the ethos of this war did not lead this combatant to distinguish between individual officers or take into account the context that one of the victims had been simply sitting at his desk and the other had been helpfully offering directions – any more than Rizzo's police seemed to distinguish between Black people going about their daily lives and those endangering public safety.

If it's war you want, authorities responded, war you shall have. Over the next five decades in prison, Russell would be beaten and disfigured, drugged to oblivion, denied medical care, and entombed in solitary confinement for a total of nearly thirty years, including the twenty-two he served consecutively. On the outside, his family would be terrorized as well.

Russell's experience, though extreme, is not unique. Prison is posited as an institution meant to contain and prevent violence, but there is hardly any form of violence in which it is not complicit. Prisons reveal what we as a people are capable of doing to one another, and they prove that we are willing to treat a great many people – over two million of them in the United States alone – as less than human.

Whatever he believed then or now, Russell's revolutionary actions as a member of the BLA did not free his people or prevent future harm. Instead, they called forth further violence from state institutions in ways that would brutalize the Shoatz family for decades to come.

At Graterford Prison, Russell was reunited with Robert Joyner, his sister Gloria's partner and a fellow co-founder of the BUC and BLA who was serving a life sentence for the Fairmount Park attack. By this point Joyner had converted to Islam and was calling himself Saeyd. He impressed on Russell his belief that "the primary reason that our collective movement

was experiencing these difficulties was due to our failure to lay a stronger foundation in the hearts and minds of ourselves and fellow revolutionaries," and that Islam was this foundation. At that time, Russell saw himself as a "foot soldier" whose job was to fight to the end rather than hash out ideas. Still, Saeyd invited him to the prison's Sunni mosque, where Russell was taken with the thoughtful and dignified proceedings. He soon converted and embarked on a study of the faith.

Bonnie brought their children to visit Russell regularly, and she converted to Islam as well. Spiritual leaders from a nearby mosque advised Russell and other incarcerated men to encourage their wives and girlfriends to "marry other men while we were in prison" because "Muslim women should have husbands who can satisfy their needs and desires." Though Russell was still very much in love with his common-law wife and did not want to lose her, he was swayed by the argument. He informed her of his decision and severed all ties. He would later deeply regret this and realize he had "inflicted a massive amount of harm to the psyches of my loved ones, from which they have not recovered to this date." Russell would have little contact with the three children he fathered with her until 2014.

Russell's siblings would sometimes take Thelma's kids to see their father. At first Theresa did not realize that the place where they visited him was a prison, but she noticed him constantly looking out the windows at the other buildings and the surrounding landscape. In hindsight, Theresa thinks that her father's main interest in their visits was to take in the view and lay plans for an escape. Russell had not yet learned to be the kind of father he would later become. He was still looking past his loved ones, searching for a chink in the walls that held him.

Becoming Maroon

In 1976, Russell was transferred to the State Correctional Institution at Huntingdon, Pennsylvania. The oldest continuously operating prison in the state, Huntingdon was known as the "breaking camp" – the place where the most incorrigible incarcerated men were sent to have their spirits (and not infrequently their bodies) broken. Russell regularly witnessed incarcerated men being clubbed to the floor by staff.

Russell and several other men resolved to escape

together and put their plan into action on September 14, 1977. They "subdued" four guards, leaving them bound in an empty cell, and used one of their keys to ascend to the roof, then threw a blanket over the top of a barbed-wire fence and climbed to freedom. Russell separated from the others immediately and ran into town until he saw the lights of a police car and hid in a crawlspace under a building. When he emerged, he realized that he had somehow fled in a circle and wound up at the front gate of the prison, where dozens of police cars were gathering to begin an organized search.

Russell backed away quietly, then fled again into the wilds of the Allegheny Mountains, driven by the sounds of the barking hounds on his trail. When at long last the sounds of the dogs moved away from him, Russell sat down behind some rocks to rest and realized that, at least for that night, "I was free!"

Russell used his training from the juvenile detention wilderness camp and the paramilitary exercises he had been doing with the BUC and BLA to survive in the mountains. He laid false trails to throw off the dogs, slept in heavy undergrowth to conceal himself, walked by moonlight, and stayed away from established trails. He was trying to head toward Raystown Lake where he and his comrades had agreed to meet if they should be separated, but once again he realized he was right back where he started near the prison. He decided to lay low where he was. For sustenance, he foraged for vegetables in local fields and at one point caught and ate a turtle raw. Despite the physical hardship, Russell found quiet joy in his life in the mountains. "I was often cold and hungry, but I felt immeasurably better off than when I was in prison."

Eventually, to gain some distance from the prison, he made a series of attempts to commandeer a vehicle, at one point leaving Dale and Marlene Rhone and their young son tied to a tree for hours after trying to steal their car, which he abandoned when it failed to restart. In another attempt, with a gun he took from the Rhones' home, he shot two bullets into a driver, Jack Powers, who got away. Finally, he took

over the car of a man named Calvin Reddings and forced him to try to speed around a police roadblock. Reddings instead leapt out of the moving car and yelled, "I'm a hostage!" Assuming Reddings to be an accomplice, the police shot at him and surrounded

SCI Huntingdon, Pennsylvania: the "breaking camp"

Russell, handcuffed him, and put him in a car where a state trooper held a shotgun under his jaw. Of this moment, Russell wrote in 2001, "Alas, the chase was over. I had been a runaway slave, but I was captured and was being returned to the plantation. It had been twenty-seven days."

Unsurprisingly, Russell's escape was received very differently inside and outside the prison. The local community, terrorized by the hostage-taking, was outraged. Russell had escaped a prison where he had been traumatized only to do the same to others. Many other incarcerated men saw in him the spirit of their ancestors who had escaped slavery, and they renamed him accordingly. When Russell had become a Muslim, he had taken the name Harun Abdul Ra'uf. Someone remarked that the police had chased Russell "like a maroon" – a term describing fugitive slaves. Maroon sounded like Harun, and the name stuck.

When he started publishing political essays, he used the name Russell Maroon Shoatz. Across the years that followed, he researched the history of maroons around the world and their valiant struggles to win and maintain their freedom. The word maroon, as defined by the *Random House Unabridged Dictionary*, evokes several other meanings applicable to his life:

> 1. to put ashore or abandon on a desolate island or coast by way of punishment . . .
>
> 2. to place in an isolated and often dangerous position
>
> 3. to abandon and to leave without aid or resources

As a noun, the word refers to a person abandoned and isolated in this way as well as to escaped slaves, "especially in mountainous areas." The irony that strikes most forcefully lies in the fact that the historical maroons stayed free or died trying, while Russell Maroon Shoatz would spend three decades in solitary confinement. Yet his adopted name is a sign of belonging to a much larger community of captives who are determined to be free.

Aftermath of the Escape

By 1977, Thelma and her children were living in a home across the street from Philadelphia's Samuel B. Huey Elementary School, where she worked and they were students. Theresa, then thirteen, had known all along that her father was in prison, and "it wasn't a bad thing, although I knew no other kids that had a family member in prison. It wasn't until my dad escaped from a prison he was at that I knew something's wrong."

As the family walked to school that morning, a reporter approached them, saying that Thelma's husband had escaped from prison and was rumored to have been seen in a nearby park. Thelma thought, "Oh my God. This is all I need." Helicopters began circling overhead.

The family arrived at school only to have it shut down and surrounded by police and FBI, presumably on the assumption that Russell would come there to see his children. All of the school children were evacuated from their classrooms but were not allowed to go home. The students and teachers crowded into the school yard, fenced in and staring at Thelma's house.

Thelma's children could see their mother, fearful and frantic, at the door to their home with police and FBI all around her, pushing their way inside, where they destroyed furniture and photographs and nearly shot the cat. They ultimately found nothing to aid them in their search for the fugitive Russell, who never had any intention of approaching Philadelphia or his family while he was on the run.

Now all of the Shoatz children's teachers, classmates, and classmates' families knew about Russell and had decided opinions about him and his family. The children were marked. Theresa was teased mercilessly by peers and teachers alike. Russell's mother tried to help protect her granddaughter from this toxic climate by arranging for Theresa to go to other schools, but the family trauma would inevitably follow her.

Russell III also struggled to process what was happening. At ten, he hadn't given his father's incarceration much thought prior to this incident, but watching the police raid his home shifted something in him. Though he bore no responsibility for his father's actions, police officers he met usually made sure he knew they recognized his name. Still, during elementary school and beyond, teachers and other loving adults in Russell III's life supported him, particularly Papa Barnes.

After the 1977 raid on their home, Thelma and her children slowly worked to restore the peace in their lives, never imagining that in three short years Russell would upend their world again.

Upon his re-arrival at Huntingdon, Russell was taken to an isolated area in the solitary confinement wing and beaten by prison staff, sustaining such severe damage to his testicles that he continues to suffer from the injury today. After this beating, Russell was kept in solitary confinement, where the guards engaged in an organized regime of harassment and abuse: "constantly coming by the cell and offering threats, keeping the lights on day and night, keeping the cell freezing cold and constantly tampering with the meager food I was given. At one point I was given a sandwich that had a heel print, with the face and paw of a cat impressed on it."

On the intervention of his lawyer, Maroon was transferred to a state prison in Pittsburgh with the promise that he would not be returned to Huntingdon, but the conditions there were similar. Russell reports that the staff kept "the level of terror so high that it would offset any ideas that any of the men were getting because of my near successful liberation attempt." Multiple times each week, several guards would don riot gear, spray mace into a cell, beat its occupant, drag him down the tier so the others could see, and deposit him in an isolation cell in the basement. The guards would tell Russell that their colleagues at Huntingdon had asked them to "take care" of him at their first opportunity. They so frequently left cigarette butts, insects, or their own spit in his food that Russell ceased eating anything that he could not buy himself from the commissary or have bought for him during visits with family and lawyers. Because he refused to eat the standard prison-issued meals, Russell received the designation of "psychiatric observation prisoner," which meant that the authorities could force him to take psychotropic medication without his consent.

After about a year of this treatment, Russell had lost considerable weight and was suffering from the stress. He started a physical altercation with his own attorney in court, which led to a judge ordering him sent to the state mental hospital for evaluation. This would become the site of his second successful escape.

Back to the Mountains

In 1978, Russell arrived at the Fairview State Hospital for the Criminally Insane. A Pulitzer Prize–winning series in the *Philadelphia Inquirer* about Fairview in 1976 revealed widespread abuse of patients at the facility. The "Fairview Findings," as the articles were called, offered evidence of overcrowding, patients beaten to death by staff, and the indiscriminate use of psychotropic medication to control behavior. Russell arrived shortly after this exposé and recalls that during his first months there, current and former members of the staff were in the process of being tried for crimes ranging from embezzlement to the murder of patients.

Russell's fellow patients – most of whom had no criminal convictions but also no other options for treatment – described the commonly used "shoe leather treatment" which involved stomping a noncompliant patient into submission or death. Because of the recent investigations, the beatings became less frequent and the extreme use of medication to control behavior had become standard practice. What the staff called "chemotherapy" kept patients nearly comatose.

The drug chlorpromazine, an antipsychotic marketed under the name Thorazine, was developed in 1954 for the treatment of hallucinations and aggressive outbursts in schizophrenic patients. Thanks to efforts to reduce mental hospital populations in the 1960s and 1970s, more and more mentally ill people

Multiple times each week, several guards would don riot gear, spray mace into a cell, beat its occupant, drag him down the tier so the others could see, and deposit him in an isolation cell in the basement.

wound up in prisons rather than hospitals, and Thorazine's use became widespread, even as its debilitating side effects became well-known. The use of Thorazine to pacify and control incarcerated people, particularly those connected to the revolutionary movements of the 1960s and 1970s, is well documented.

Russell's nightly dose was administered at 8 p.m., and he would stumble through the next morning, not feeling like he had regained clarity and equilibrium until about 1 p.m. He watched other men lie on benches in a semicomatose state all day long and feared that this would be his future if he remained medicated. One night after taking Thorazine, Russell fainted. He had been given an overdose. Russell spent two days in intensive care. After this, when his nightly doses began again, he devised a way to hold the medicine in his mouth and then secretly spit it out.

By this point, Russell had become romantically involved with a young college student named Oshun (legal name Phyllis Hill), who visited him regularly to talk about Black liberation. Together they began planning an escape and enlisted the help of Russell's friend and fellow patient Lumumba (legal name Clifford Futch). Oshun started stockpiling weapons.

On March 2, 1980, Oshun came to visit wearing heavy winter clothing that concealed a submachine gun and a revolver. Russell and Lumumba used the weapons Oshun had brought to force patients, staff, and visitors against the wall and make their escape. Oshun led Russell and Lumumba to a place where she and her friends had deposited provisions to last them a month in the wilderness. The trio packed all of their gear onto a sled and headed through the snow into the Appalachian Mountains. The plan was to stay away from all contact with other people for about a month and wait for the authorities to call off the search. Eventually, a friend would deliver a car that they could drive to a new life underground.

After two nights of camping in the snow, several of Lumumba's fingers showed signs of frostbite. The group realized they might have to head back to civilization to find medical treatment. Meanwhile, a trapper spotted Russell and alerted the police.

The three fugitives fled with their guns up the mountain to an outcropping of rocks that could serve as a kind of bunker. The crackle of police radios soon alerted them that their pursuers had arrived. The fugitives opened fire, which the police returned. Chunks of bark dislodged by bullets rained down into the bunker. The authorities offered to send a reporter, a lawyer, or an FBI agent to talk to them, but Russell rejected each attempt at negotiations. About two hours into this standoff, Oshun told Russell and Lumumba she was ready to surrender. They called out to the authorities to hold their fire so she could emerge with her hands up. Once she was out in the open, unarmed, a negotiator demanded that Russell and Lumumba surrender as well. They decided they had to do so or risk watching Oshun be gunned down. They joined her with their hands raised.

As reporters and police buzzed around them, Russell discovered that the police had set up an ambush right behind their bunker. If Oshun had not led them to surrender when they did, they would almost certainly have been killed by a volley of bullets from behind. More than fifty police and FBI agents had been involved in the shootout. Miraculously, no one had been injured or killed.

Organizing from the Inside

Russell and Lumumba were sent to solitary confinement at the State Correctional Institution at Dallas, Pennsylvania, where they went on a hunger strike in an attempt to get transferred into the general population. Six or seven other men joined them for a time. The authorities shuffled the two through several moves to county jails and back to Fairview, keeping them at separate facilities in an attempt to break their resolve. Eventually, they both landed back in solitary at SCI Dallas, where they again rallied other men

to join them in the hunger strike, which ultimately lasted for fifty-five days. Russell and Lumumba decided to call off the strike before it killed them, but not before Russell had once again demonstrated that he was both strong-willed and inspiring to other incarcerated men.

Oshun spent time in a county jail in Philadelphia where she was housed with women from the MOVE political organization (whose residential headquarters would be bombed a few years later in 1985 by the Philadelphia Police Department, killing six adults and five children). She agreed to a plea deal that would give her a reduced sentence if she agreed to keep a low profile with the media. The New York BLA had freed Assata Shakur from a prison in New Jersey in late 1979, and the authorities did not want another revolutionary Black woman to capture headlines. Oshun was not required to testify against Russell and Lumumba. She served just under three years in prison for her role in their escape.

Russell and Lumumba decided to represent themselves in their court cases. At trial, Russell summoned Philadelphia police and FBI agents to testify about his long history of political actions. He used the Freedom of Information Act to obtain copies of FBI documents showing that J. Edgar Hoover's Bureau had kept a file on him and targeted him as an urban guerrilla. These tactics did not ultimately sway the jury, however, and he received his second life sentence. Lumumba met the same fate. The two were returned to SCI Dallas and placed in solitary confinement with no clear end date. Their cells were searched by guards every day, despite the fact that they had no contact with anyone who could bring them contraband. This went on for more than a year.

One day another man in solitary, Sly, refused to be handcuffed so that the guards could administer his cell's daily search. A squad of officers in riot gear attacked him and dragged him, covered in blood, down to an even more isolated part of the prison, known as the dungeon. This event caused such a stir among the men in solitary that they demanded to see a shift commander to register a complaint. When this went nowhere, Russell led the men in a riot. In the fight, prison staff nearly cut off one of Russell's fingers. Russell was handcuffed, beaten, stripped naked, hauled to the dungeon, and left for several hours. A medical attendant came later that evening and sent

Russell to the prison hospital, where his finger was stitched back in place.

Russell was transferred yet again to solitary at Pittsburgh, where he began another hunger strike that others joined. In court, a lawyer successfully argued that the charges against Russell and the other rioters should be dismissed because they had been consistently terrorized by the guards.

After this victory, Russell discovered that the men at Pittsburgh had taken up the hunger strike again and devised a strategy to keep it going for long periods of time. Two or three men would refuse to eat for about twenty days before another set of strikers would take over. In the meantime, those who were eating would write letters to activists and media outlets to draw attention to the plight of those in perpetual solitary confinement. This enabled the men to collectively maintain the hunger strike for about a year and attract the attention of the host of a radio show, the NAACP, and enough activists to hold several demonstrations outside the prison. After the prison banned people who had been seen protesting from visiting their incarcerated loved ones, activists staged a march where everyone wore ski masks to protect their identities. Prison administrators eventually relented, allowing protesters to visit their loved ones again and moving out all of the men who had been held in indefinite solitary confinement.

As soon as Russell was released from solitary confinement, he began organizing men serving life sentences into a political body. Lifers and those with decades-long sentences tend to stabilize any prison population because they have reason to invest in their community's well-being across time. Even compared to the rest of the United States, where sentences tend to be harsher than those in other countries, Pennsylvania is extraordinarily punitive in its sentencing. Russell had the misfortune of being

Russell Shoatz's 1980 court filing in his own defense arguing for status as a prisoner of war

not just from Pennsylvania but from Philadelphia County, which has sent a higher proportion of its people to prison for life without parole than the overall incarceration rates of 140 nations.

In March 1982, the men at SCI Pittsburgh formed an organization called the Pennsylvania Association of Lifers (PAL) with the goal of lobbying for the end of life without parole sentences. The organization grew from twelve members to one hundred after Russell got involved, and when they held their first election, Russell was unanimously chosen as their president. At the same time, PAL voted in a board of directors. A few hours after the votes were tallied, Russell and the entire board were rounded up by guards and sent to solitary. The lifers were prepared: they had documentation that they had formed their group in compliance with all prison regulations on the creation of inmate clubs. According to Russell, guards ransacked the cells of all the men they had just placed in solitary and destroyed all paperwork they found. However, he had anticipated this possibility and left a copy of PAL's papers with a man who was not on the club's board. When the prison charged Russell and the rest of the PAL leadership with holding unauthorized meetings, this man produced the necessary records to refute those accusations.

The authorities then changed tactics and accused Russell and the board members of creating PAL to conduct illegal activities inside the prison. Though no evidence was presented to corroborate these charges, Russell and his colleagues were all punished with six

A solitary confinement cell (Rikers Island, New York). The size of the cells in which Shoatz was held continuously from 1991 to 2014 was ca. 64 to 80 square feet.

months in solitary. The original election results were discarded, but while their leadership sat in solitary, the voting lifers responded by reelecting Russell and selected temporary appointees to carry out PAL's activities until its leadership returned to general population. The lifers engaged a lawyer and even sued the prison administration when it once again disbanded the organization, but lost in court.

To judge by the harsh response, nothing Russell had done in his life until now posed such a threat to Pennsylvania's prison system as did his role in democratically and legally founding an inmate club. Neither his physical attacks on prison staff nor his multiple escapes brought about such a sustained

and relentless regime of punishment. Russell's time in solitary became an indeterminate sentence with perfunctory reviews and rejections every thirty days. He would not find any relief for the next seven years, and when he did, it came because the authorities erroneously concluded that he was involved in instigating a prison rebellion at SCI Camp Hill about which he had no knowledge and which happened over two hundred miles away. Though he played no part in the rebellion, Russell was flagged as suspect and sent to the US federal prison in Leavenworth, Kansas.

This proved fortunate. In Leavenworth, federal authorities moved Russell out of solitary confinement and into the general prison population after his supporters challenged Pennsylvania's claims about his involvement in the Camp Hill riot. For a little over a year, he had a welcome respite from life in solitary, was able to see much more of his family, and met many other incarcerated revolutionaries, including Leonard Peltier of the American Indian Movement, Sundiata Acoli of the BLA, and Phil Africa of MOVE. These months in the federal system would be Russell's last taste of regular social interaction for more than two decades. When the Pennsylvania state authorities had him moved back into their prisons in 1991, they put him back in solitary and almost literally threw away the key. He would remain in perpetual solitary confinement for the next twenty-two years.

The Hole

The inciting incident for Russell's first seven-year stretch in "the hole," as both guards and incarcerated people refer to solitary confinement, was not one of his escapes but rather his election as president of PAL; presumably, the next twenty-two years were simply a continuation of this punishment. The Pennsylvania Department of Corrections continued to conduct perfunctory reviews of his status while offering no hope that it would be lifted. In 2013, after Russell had spent more than two decades in solitary, the prison superintendent justified keeping him there because, as Victoria Law wrote in *The Nation*, he had been a part of "radical militant groups, his former association with the Black Panther Party, and his current political views and activities via mail and phone, his ability to organize others." None of these arguments had ever previously been presented to Russell, his family, or his lawyers, who believe that prison authorities saw Russell's leadership capacity and political beliefs as more threatening than his past actions.

Russell's life in the hole consisted of twenty-three hours locked in his cell each day, with the lights always on. He could leave only to take a ten-minute shower three times a week and go to an enclosed cage by himself for one hour five times a week. The cost of each foray out of his cell was to be strip-searched, handcuffed, and shackled. Russell's family could visit him for one hour per week, driving seven hours each way to speak to him through Plexiglas. Russell could receive letters but could not have books or periodicals mailed to him. He could not keep personal books with him beyond legal materials and one religious text. He could request up to two books per week from the prison library, but he could not read anything not already owned by the prison.

Despite these constraints, Russell embarked on an energetic project of self-education. He dove into anything that he could get his hands on – "economics, education, entertainment, labor, law, politics, religion, and warfare" – particularly anything that touched on liberation struggles throughout history. In the early years, he organized seminars in his cell block to discuss these readings and ideas, which even included "more than a few prison guards – once they got over the idea that we prisoners could not intelligently interact with them." Though, being in solitary, participants had to remain in their cells, they hollered up and down the hall and passed around handwritten missives by "fishing lines" through the bars.

"As the hardened young men would be sent to the hole, my comrades and I would immediately engage them about why they were in prison and stress how important it was that they educate themselves before leaving. It was literally a mental boot camp," he writes. Like his long-ago gang interventions, "As part of my mission I have also dedicated my life to trying to help guide the youth of the present generation away from the traps that ensnared me, and helping them find their own mission in life."

An unexpected result of all this was that he discovered the writings of radical feminists that caused him to realize how much of the world and his own view of it was founded in misogyny. He had flattered himself that he left this behind after his gangster days, but, as he wrote in a 2010 essay, "after becoming politically conscious, I further deluded myself into believing that being a 'revolutionary' made me a champion dedicated to the uplifting of all humanity. It turned out, however, that I had just transferred many of my woman-hating practices to another arena. That's the

Russell has cumulatively spent nearly thirty years in solitary confinement, which he describes as "social torture paid for with tax dollars."

special fate of male revolutionaries who put so much stock in the testosterone-dominated armed struggle." He applied himself to a serious self-examination and heartily recommended "matriarchal" philosophy to others.

As the years went on, the walls closed in. He was transferred to SCI Greene, a new "supermax" prison with a "control unit" designed to inflict sensory deprivation, with solid doors sealed against fishing and soundproofed against hollering. The rules were tightened and more harshly enforced, and the literature available to read was drastically reduced. Russell and company creatively responded to these new conditions by writing out their thoughts and mailing them to supporters on the outside, who in turn mailed them back inside the prison to the intended recipients, but once this practice was discovered the mail room put a stop to it. Even then, Russell continued writing essays for the outside world, but he felt acutely the loss of this last form of human interaction.

Year after year in the hole sent Russell into profound spirals of depression. He could not get out of bed some days and spent much time contemplating ways to kill himself. Ultimately, the only reason he did not end his life was that he had no way to do so.

Juan Méndez, the former United Nations Special Rapporteur on Torture, asserts that more than fifteen days of solitary confinement constitutes torture. Méndez interviewed Russell in 2015 and characterized the conditions of his life in the hole as "cruel, inhuman, or degrading punishment under customary international law standards." Russell has cumulatively spent nearly thirty years in solitary confinement, which he describes as "social torture paid for with tax dollars."

In 2013, Russell filed a lawsuit to end his indefinite isolation and was released into the general population in 2014 on the condition that he not do any further political organizing. He was awarded a $99,000 settlement in 2016 for his pain and suffering

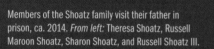
Members of the Shoatz family visit their father in prison, ca. 2014. *From left:* Theresa Shoatz, Russell Maroon Shoatz, Sharon Shoatz, and Russell Shoatz III.

in solitary. Russell divided the settlement money between Thelma and Bonnie, the mothers of his children, in a highly delayed form of child support. Even now, he says, he is still learning to be a father and grandfather.

Parenting from Prison

All of Russell's seven children are now in their fifties, and each of them has had to get to know him through prison visits, letters, and brief phone calls. Russell makes the most of these opportunities and loves interacting with his children, who have impressed him by becoming accomplished and caring adults despite, or perhaps because of, their challenges in life.

Theresa takes pride in the lessons she has learned from her father and has repeatedly sought his mentorship. She credits her father with encouraging her to take in twenty-eight foster children and to create afterschool programming for students with incarcerated parents. She was venting to him about kids acting out at the school where she worked, and he prodded her, "Why don't you do something about it?" He told her to be for them what she had needed somebody to be for her while he was gone. "I ended up loving those kids like my own," she says.

As an adult, Russell III got to know Russell chiefly through political and intellectual debates as they sat together in prison visiting rooms. "These conversations with my father have been like mentally battling one of the greatest mixed martial arts fighters of all time," he says, a one-on-one reprise of Russell's seminars with other incarcerated men. The two have challenged each other and grown in their respect for the other's perspectives, even when they disagree. Russell III came to understand the youthful version of his father as "ready to dedicate his life to the movement, to the salvation of his people."

Russell III does not believe that the BLA's violent tactics were effective or morally sound. He believes that Black people and others who endure incarceration, injustice in the courts, and police brutality and murder have the right and need to respond, but that more violence will not solve this problem. He said in a 2020 joint interview with his father:

I've spent forty years learning from my father's struggles. We don't see eye-to-eye on all topics related to our people's fight for liberation. But when it comes to character, courage, commitment, and critical thinking, I must admit that those disgruntled teachers, authority figures, and police officers from my youth were spot on: I *have* proudly ended up being just like my father – and my father deserves to be free.

Russell III and his sisters have devoted much of their adult lives to seeking their father's release. They have led teams of activists, lawyers, scholars, artists, and figures in popular culture – among them Chuck D, Mos Def, and Colin Kaepernick – to lobby for him.

In recent years, Russell has had reason to feel greater urgency about both his liberation and his ability to connect with his family. He has a terminal cancer diagnosis and knows he will not receive adequate health care as long as he remains in prison.

People in prison have the right to receive medical treatment, but they often cannot access it. The Prison Policy Initiative found that "mass incarceration has shortened the overall US life expectancy by five years." Russell's cancer led to the removal of both his upper and lower intestines. He now lives with a colostomy bag and has endured several debilitating rounds of chemotherapy. Meanwhile, he caught and survived Covid-19.

In April 2021, he was informed that his cancer was aggressive and terminal, and that the prison would not offer him palliative treatment. He appealed for a medical release to live out his few remaining days with his family, and the court denied him on August 12, 2021. When I received this news, all I could think was of Toni Morrison's refrain in *Song of Solomon*: "Everybody wants the life of a Black man." When I emailed my condolences to Russell, he responded with the indomitable attitude that is characteristic of him, insisting that he would petition the court again at a later date.

Reckoning with Violence

The Shoatz children's loss of these years with their father and their grief and anxiety at having a parent very ill in prison have weighed heavily on me as I have come to know them and their story. For the twenty years that my own father was in prison, I lived a version of this, too. In a professional capacity, I have worked for many years with families of the incarcerated and seen firsthand the way the prison system treats us. I see the vast discrepancy between the price incarcerated people pay for the crimes of which they are convicted and the price the prisons, police, district attorneys, judges, FBI agents, and politicians who run "get tough on crime" campaigns never pay for the harm they cause these human beings and their families. Most government actors who contribute to the suffering of a family like the Shoatzes do what they do in the name of justice, yet they seldom see the practical effects of their actions in the lives of others. If these authorities pride themselves on how

> **If these authorities pride themselves on how well the system works, that is because they have defined justice in their own terms without asking Thelma or the Shoatz children what justice might look like in their lives.**

well the system works, that is because they have defined justice in their own terms without asking Thelma or the Shoatz children what justice might look like in their lives. These authorities often respond to the victims of violence meted out by one government agency by telling them to seek relief from yet another government agency, and seem unconcerned when the bureaucratic mechanism fails to provide it. For many families like the Shoatzes, this is what due process looks like.

The prisons in which Russell has lived for the last five decades have spent enormous sums of public money to discipline him and contain his potential for violence. Meanwhile, their own violence against Russell and other incarcerated people – and the police brutality against Blacks and other oppressed people that he originally sought to oppose – did not receive the same level of scrutiny or accountability.

The revolutionaries of the 1960s and 1970s were asking for this accountability, using tactics that were neither blameless nor effective. Like Russell, many of the men and women who took extreme political actions in those decades remain in prison. They risked their own lives and took the lives of others because they wanted the world to be radically different. Neither violent nor nonviolent revolution came. Instead, the United States built the largest prison system in world history and invested in military-grade weapons to police its cities.

Any act of violence creates a dissonance that

cannot be fixed. There is something incomplete and incompletable about the aftermath of a violent event. This story neither begins nor ends with Russell. His rage and humiliation are products of hundreds of years of oppression that cannot be fully told, as well as the specific brutality that Russell witnessed in his neighborhood. The prisons in which Russell has lived have been hellholes from which any person would want desperately to escape, but that, too, came at extraordinary cost to others.

The argument for human decency toward incarcerated people should not depend upon their innocence or guilt.

One way to try to parse the incredible volume and magnitude of this tragedy is to list the kinds of violence that Russell has committed and those that have been committed against him. The lists would be long and twisting and not balance one another out in either direction, an infinite regression of trauma and retribution. The argument for human decency toward incarcerated people should not depend upon their innocence or guilt. Even if one assumes the absolute worst about Russell Shoatz and his motives, nothing justifies the ongoing violence against him and his family.

Russell Maroon Shoatz has spent nearly half a century in prison. He was twenty-nine years old when he went to prison and is now seventy-eight. Neither he nor any one of us could possibly be the same person we were forty-nine years ago. A man nearing his eighth decade of life with a terminal diagnosis and a colostomy bag is not a danger to society. Letting Russell die in prison is how a vengeful society tries to resolve the trauma of his actions, but in the end it's just one more act of violence and humiliation against a Black man. The only decent path forward is to send this man home.

Absences, Gaps, and Loose Ends

In the story I've told here, the experiences of the crime victims, their families, and their communities remain a vast lacuna. They too deserve a thorough and thoughtful consideration of their experiences, if that is something they desire. Their lives were

undoubtedly as radically shaped by Russell Shoatz's actions as was his own. Over the years, Russell III and the Shoatz family, as well as journalists and others, have reached out to the victims' families and found that they did not want to have a conversation about Russell and his case. They need not be called upon again to air their pain and grief in public if they do not wish it. The Von Colln family wanted the Philadelphia Five, including Russell, to receive the death penalty in their original sentencing. In a 2016 news story in the *Philadelphia Inquirer,* Kurt Von Colln, son of the murdered sergeant and a retired Philadelphia police officer himself, rejected Russell III's overture to the victims' families: "No way. This guy doesn't deserve it," he said. Russell Shoatz "has taken a lot away from the Von Colln family."

In a strange twist, at least two members of Russell's immediate family ended up going into law enforcement. Russell and Bonnie's son Hassan spent four years in the Marine Corps, and when he left the military, he wrote to his father in prison and asked Russell how he would feel if Hassan joined the Washington, DC, police. Russell told me, "I ENCOURAGED him to follow through on that, as by then it was CLEAR to me MORE could be accomplished WITHIN the system." This surprised me more than anything else Russell said.

Russell and Thelma's daughter Tammy became a prison guard in Virginia. Daughter and father started corresponding to get to know one another better, and at some point, she asked him to send her material about the Black Panthers to share with the incarcerated people in her institution. He was happy to oblige.

In this, as in so many other ways, Russell's life resists neat classification. He is both a man who has done some terrible things and a man who has been terrorized by powerful institutions. He is not the same person he once was, and his politics have shifted in some key ways. One would not expect a member of the BLA to become the supportive father of a police officer and a prison guard.

The other members of the Shoatz family have consistently sought lives of peace, despite the violence that has so deeply marked their stories. Theresa transformed the pain of her childhood into compassion for other children with incarcerated parents. Russell III rejected designating anyone the enemy and carried forward the love he shared with his "two fathers." Thelma, battered on all sides and placed in an impossible position, rose up for her children and found refuge in prayer. Russell reached out of solitary confinement with his writing. He has told difficult truths about himself and others and tried to speak for ways that we might build a world with greater justice and equality for oppressed peoples. He is always learning, always trying to grow beyond the many kinds of walls that have confined him.

What Peace Requires

Peace, that most elusive of goals, is often preached to the powerless and the marginalized when in reality the powerful must make the largest move. As I've worked on this story for the past eight months, several truths have come home to me. A genuine commitment to peace and public safety does not look like a gunman at your door – be that a political revolutionary or a police officer. In order to reckon meaningfully with violence and move toward something better, we must mourn deeply all of these tragedies: the murder of Sergeant Frank Von Colln, the extraordinary suffering of Patrolman James Harrington, the torture of Russell Maroon Shoatz, the abuse of Thelma Christian, the homelessness of her children, and all the suffering of others connected to this story. Not one of these lives has less value than another. Rage condemns us all, whether it is the rage of the police or the Black Liberation Army. The most difficult and valuable revolution is sustained peace.

Papa Barnes believes that an intervention could be made in the police force to stop some of the violence. He says everyone on the force knows who is "not doing their job" and that commanding officers should be able to report those who are committing acts of brutality and not be reprimanded for doing so. Barnes believes that this kind of strategy could have prevented the death of George Floyd, because Derrick Chauvin had previously shown signs that he was the kind of officer who would do such a thing. Barnes's ideas to reform policing are noble and humane, but it will take much more widespread interest and commitment from the police, courts, and lawmakers to end the murders of unarmed citizens or the persistent harassment of many in minority communities. Despite his courage, a good police officer like Papa Barnes could not protect Russell III from the same humiliation that his father endured on the streets.

All the same, Papa Barnes and his work in community policing have made a significant impact

Photograph by Melinda Goodwin/*Plough*

Russell Shoatz III and the author speak at a *Plough* event on August 7, 2021.

in the lives of individuals. Barnes says, "I'm not trying to change the world. I'll take it one person at a time, like Russell III is my son." The current police commissioner of Philadelphia is another "adopted daughter" he met through church. In every interaction he had as a police officer in his community, Barnes says, he tried to be fair and to walk in this world in love. While he did not manage to change the system, he has been a strong presence for peace in his community for decades, both on and off the force.

Now a full-time pastor of a nondenominational church since retiring from the police, Barnes is more concerned for Russell's soul than his physical health, and wants him to offer a sincere apology without expectation of how it will be received. He prays for Russell and for the victims and their families. He hopes each of them may shed whatever hatred has lived in their hearts and that they find healing and forgiveness. He also hopes and prays that those energized to fight racism and injustice today (as well they should be) seek solutions that do not further the cycle of violence.

Thelma says she had to work hard to wade through the violence that surrounded her family and not lose her mind. She wants "the light of goodness to reflect on my children" and for them to know that they and their father were something more than the crimes he may have committed. As difficult as her relationship with her husband has been and though she does not communicate with him, Thelma remains married to Russell to this day. She does not believe that any person should serve as many years in prison as he has. Her mother encouraged her to pray for Russell, and though Thelma felt resistant at first, she started including her husband in her daily prayers. She now forgives Russell for all the harm he caused her, though she struggled with this for a long time. "I never forgot what he did, and I think I never will forget it. But I've learned that it doesn't help me to carry hate for him." Independently of this decision on her part, Russell asked me to make this message public: "To Thelma Shoatz, I offer her SPECIAL APOLO-GIES for having physically beat and abused her."

Though he first converted to Islam back in 1972, Russell tells me that it is only in the past four or five years that he has been practicing in earnest, finding spiritual meaning beyond any political utility. Central to this practice is a reconsideration of the actions of his life. "I HURT a LOT of people (relations and otherwise). Now I've vowed to do NO MORE HARM, and seek ATONEMENT from ALL those I've HARMED! And FORGIVENESS from Allah (the Creator)."
In this, too, he has decided to take full ownership, sending me this message on June 13, 2021:

> I would like for you to place MY acknowledge-ments of having harmed MANY people in my life – my family and ALL those outside of that circle, including Philadelphia, PA, Fairmount Park Police Sgt. Frank Von Colln, who was killed on Aug. 29, 1970, and Fairmount Park Police Officer James Harrington, who was shot and severely wounded during the same incident, as well as Jack Powers, whom I shot in an attempt to steal his truck after my escape from prison in 1977. My misdirected rage and racial humiliation played a part, but MY actions were WRONG!!! I here offer APOLOGIES to ALL those mentioned, and BEG for FORGIVENESS!!!

This statement cannot bring back what was lost. In writing it, however, Russell gestures, as does anyone who sincerely apologizes, toward a more humane world, a world *after* conflict. I struggle to imagine what a similar collective and institutional taking of responsibility for the harm done to him and his family would even look like. Russell has always had a strong capacity to imagine a way out, a way into a world that does not yet exist. In this, we have much to learn from him.

In correspondence, Russell typically signs off with either "In solidarity" or "Straight ahead!" These two directives point the way forward, reminding us that no one's freedom exists in isolation but only in solidarity with all people as we strive toward a justice we have yet to realize. ➤

For more on the sources used in this article, see Plough.com/ShoatzSources.

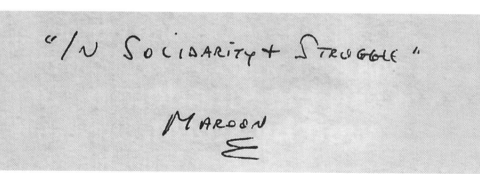

Kay Leverton,
*Barn Owl
Landing*,
scraperboard

For the Celts

Hart Island, New York, April 2020

To whom it may concern: leave them their rings—
those sentimental claddaghs pledging love,
friendship and loyalty; enduring things
that might scorch ash in a nameless, kinless grave.
Those daytime drones will pass overhead.
Then from night's watchful edifice a quill
will rain—not on the ceased, but on the dead.
If only there should lie a poet whose words prevail.
But know for those remotely Celtic—for the throng
of voiceless, faceless, buried without coins
for passage but with proffered hearts—dark's song
will come. Then pray the *cailleach-oidhche bhàn*'s
forgotten scream might raise them; and unleash
their shimmering green dancers, *Na Fir-chlis*.

cailleach-oidhche bhàn: white hag of the night, barn owl
Na Fir-chlis: the Merry Dancers, aurora borealis.

MHAIRI OWENS

Child *of* *the* Stars

✫

Le Petit Prince lands in Bolivia.

RIVER CLAURE

River Claure is a Bolivian visual artist and creator of Warawar Wawa, *a photography project that reimagines Antoine de Saint-Exupéry's* Le Petit Prince *as an Aymara fairy tale. Plough's Coretta Thomson caught up with him to find out the story behind it. She introduces their conversation:*

IN THE ART HISTORY COURSES I took at the University of Montevideo, our professors often spoke of transculturation, a term that anthropologist Fernando Ortiz used to describe the blending of several cultures to create something new. It's a phenomenon that's been glaringly obvious to me wherever I've traveled in Latin America. Unlike the European colonists of what is now the United States who displaced, erased, and replaced the First Nations, Castilian conquistadors generally took the helm of the pre-Columbian world order – often violently, and to their own profit – adding Christian and European elements to it. The legacy of these practices is certainly mixed, but mestizo art and architecture are among the most beautiful results.

So I was intrigued to hear of a contemporary example of transculturation: *Warawar Wawa*, a reinterpretation of Antoine de Saint-Exupéry's *Le Petit Prince* in a twenty-first-century Bolivian context, which illustrates the first Aymara version of this classic translated directly from the French. I spoke with its creator, River Claure, a photographer and Cochabamba native, on Zoom. An urbanite of both Aymara and Caucasian heritage, he read the novella for the first time on the Madrid metro, while studying visual arts. The text spoke to him but the blond protagonist in the illustrations was clearly created for a different context. How would an Andean Little Prince look, he wondered, and what characters would he meet on a journey through Latin America?

After returning to Bolivia, Claure completed several small projects to discover his style while securing support for the *Le Petit Prince* project. As he explained:

> Today, we are all one big mix of cultures and races, but for some strange reason extremist discourses are dominant in many parts of the world. I, for one, do some things the Indigenous way – like wearing traditional sandals and chewing coca leaf – but I also watch Netflix and drink Coca-Cola. Sociologist Silvia Rivera Cusicanqui coined a term which I love: *ch'ixi*, loosely translated as "gray." It refers to the Aymara weaving method used to make *aguayo* blankets: when one color is juxtaposed over another, a third, indeterminate hue is created. I believe we are all *ch'ixi*, and I strive to explore this reality in my work.

Eventually, the national government offered to finance *Warawar Wawa*. After a year of preparation, Claure and his team traveled through the Andes for a month, taking photographs. Claure reflects on the project, which was published last year:

> *Le Petit Prince* is an adult book disguised as a children's story; it touches deeply on themes like love, friendship, and death. It was a challenge to rethink these themes in a modern Bolivian setting. Although the Aymara culture was once very close to nature, the polarization of the last decades has changed things dramatically. Things are labeled as either Indigenous and rural, or urban and foreign, with a clear line between them. I attribute this to the centuries of mistreatment the Aymara suffered, a wound that was still fresh when the Indigenous came to power. Instead of cultivating the ancestral, nonviolent culture of the villages, a new sentiment emerged, one of getting back at the urbanites, Whites, and the children of immigrants.
>
> So this project was not so much a reflection of modern Bolivia as an invitation to reconciliation. It has been very well received, which I think means that many people identify with it. I believe that using art to help people see themselves as *ch'ixi*, highlighting our similarities and equal worth, chips away at the barrier that has divided us for so long. Change will only come when we imagine and work for a better nation: living alongside each other, loving and embracing Indigenous culture but also the West's positive contributions.

This interview, from December 8, 2020, was conducted and translated from the Spanish by Coretta Thomson.

Excerpts from Antoine de Saint Exupéry, *The Little Prince*, trans. Richard Howard (Mariner Books, Houghton Mifflin Harcourt, 2000). Used by permission.

"The literal translation of *petit prince* in Aymara is *pirincipitu wawa*, meaning 'baby prince.' In speaking with the team of Native translators, however, we realized that there is no reference for monarchy in Aymara culture. So we went for an interesting word: *warawar*, which refers to a constellation, a group of lakes in the Andes, or a group of mountains; in sum, a group of superior beings. So *Warawar Wawa* means 'child who descended from something magical and fantastic.'"

—River Claure

From *Le Petit Prince*:

"What makes the desert beautiful," the little prince said, "is that it hides a well somewhere . . ."

"The King is reimagined as a Virgin of the Mountain of Potosí, a seventeenth-century baroque icon. I consider both King and Virgin to be figures of power in the Spanish culture that conquered the Americas. It also gives a nod to mestizo art and transculturation: she's a Pachamama – the Mother Earth the Aymaras venerated – with foreign features. We placed shiny stones on the slopes of the mound to represent the gold and silver that has been extracted from Cerro Potosí over almost five hundred years. Bricks are included because Bolivia's industry was born here too: the first railroad and coal-fired machinery in the country were used at these mines. The queen's head is ringed with fireworks that are often used in Aymara festivals today, like a golden crown for the Virgin."

—River Claure

"Instead of professional actors, I like to hire local people from the communities where I do the photo shoots. But we did do a casting call for the Little Prince himself. It was in El Alto, on the outskirts of La Paz, and hundreds of boys came; a few girls even showed up! Finally, we chose this young boy of Aymara descent. We traveled with him and his mother all over the Andes for a month, and became very close. We read the original *Le Petit Prince* together and planned the takes as a team; it was very beautiful and collaborative."

—*River Claure*

From *Le Petit Prince*:

"Only the children know what they are looking for," said the little prince. "They spend their time on a rag doll and it becomes very important, and if it's taken away from them, they cry . . . "

From *Le Petit Prince:*

"My flower is ephemeral," the little prince said to himself, "and she has only four thorns with which to defend herself against the world! And I've left her all alone where I live!"

"The rose is the character I had the hardest time to conceptualize, but I'm happy with the result. Some literary critics consider her a symbol of sexual awakening, but for me, the rose is a motherly figure. After all, the first woman a child loves is his mother! And if you invert the image of a woman in a skirt, her dress looks like an open flower. So here you see a *cholita,* a traditional woman boxer, portraying the rose that defends herself with her thorns. But she is also an important part of the child's world, an object of his love. At one point in the story the prince realizes that there are many other roses besides his mother, but she is still the most beautiful one in his eyes."

—*River Claure*

The Rose Garden appears on the opening spread.

For more on
River Claure's
Warawar Wawa
project, see the
artist's website at
riverclaure.com. ⇀

Editors' Picks

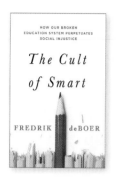

The Cult of Smart
How Our Broken Education System Perpetuates Injustice

Fredrik deBoer
(All Points Books)

Kurt Vonnegut's classic 1961 short story "Harrison Bergeron" pictures a supposedly utopian version of the United States in which strict equality is enforced through the use of mandated handicaps such as earpieces that transmit piercing sounds to disrupt thought for those with above-average intelligence. Few of us would take our commitment to equality to such lengths. Yet many of us do view equality – of opportunity and outcome – as something worth approximating as a benchmark for justice in our society. But is such equality achievable, and is it even necessary for the well-being and flourishing of all?

Fredrik deBoer's *The Cult of Smart* complicates this question by forcing us to consider the limits of education as a viable path to full equality. Even if we implemented all the education reforms imaginable, deBoer argues, we would still have undeniable variance in individual natural intelligence and aptitude, which would lead to disparate outcomes. DeBoer asserts that if we are serious about justice, we need to take seriously the fact that natural intelligence is not equally distributed. Given this inequality, one's degree of natural intelligence is not an appropriate basis for assigning value or determining who gets to live the good life any more than race or some other contingent factor of human existence.

DeBoer further argues that our current economic system suppresses these truths in favor of commitment to the ideology of meritocracy (itself a term coined in Michael Young's 1958 dystopia *The Rise of the Meritocracy*). Whereas Vonnegut's dystopia seeks to blur or remove all distinctions in ability and talent, meritocracy justifies those distinctions in ways that undermine any sense of solidarity. Specifically, meritocracy allows us to take credit for our luck (having a natural aptitude for academics, for example) as though it were our virtue, while blaming others for their lack of luck as though it were a vice. Just as insidiously, meritocracy seduces those committed to social justice to focus on facilitating upward mobility within the current economic system rather than changing the status quo to something that better serves the needs of everyone regardless of their abilities. Thus, while neither deBoer's nor Vonnegut's work should be read as an attack on progressive efforts to achieve greater equality of outcome, both invite readers to question the assumption that equality of opportunity should be the basis for individual and communal wellbeing.

Once we step away from that assumption, we can begin envisioning a society in which everyone, regardless of intelligence or talent, is valued and can experience the fullest possible flourishing. One of the worst features of the world of Harrison Bergeron is the impoverishment of the fine arts. Such a loss is also present in approaches to education focused exclusively on utilitarian ends, such as workforce development. If we could reject the cult of smart and develop an education system that supports and rewards everyone, there would also be more room for the pursuit of beauty, truth, and goodness.

—*Anthony M. Barr*

The Utopians
Six Attempts to Build the Perfect Society

Anna Neima
(Picador)

The interwar period of the 1920s and '30s saw an explosion all over the world of groups establishing radical utopian communities as alternatives to the capitalist and nationalist projects that had resulted in the Great War and its devastations. In her new book, Anna Neima explores six of these groups, including the Bruderhof communities founded by Eberhard and Emmy Arnold.

Neima presents a vivid picture of the early Bruderhof movement. The Arnolds' simple appeal to living as the first Christians did – holding everything in common, resisting violence, and practicing radical hospitality – was something others found deeply alluring. This would eventually lead them to a fifteen-room house in the German village of Sannerz in 1920. The community was magnetic, representing not just a biblical ideal but a reality, and in the following year it attracted 2500 national and international visitors – Christians, Jews, socialists, pacifists, freethinkers, and others.

Community life was not without its difficulties. Besides the issue of finding enough space and food for all those visitors and new members, Neima highlights the Arnolds' informal, faith-based approach to finances. Their expectation that God would provide what was needed when it was needed resulted in a chunk of the community's membership splitting off. Add to this the rise of Nazism and the deep suspicion the Bruderhof's values aroused among government officials.

Ironically, it was during this time that the community experienced some of its greatest growth. Eberhard met with an early death in 1935, but Emmy would go with the community to Liechtenstein, England, Paraguay, and eventually the United States.

Neima takes some liberties with her source material, and a few inaccuracies surface in her account. Nonetheless, her extensive knowledge of utopian projects – not just in the 1920s and '30s but in the broader history of the modern world – results in a compelling and informative narrative that situates each group in this unique historical moment.

Besides the Bruderhof movement, Neima explores Rabindranath Tagore's communities in rural Bengal; Dorothy and Leonard Elmhirst's Dartington Hall in Devon, England; Mushanokōji Saneatsu's Atarashiki-mura in the mountains of Kyūshū, Japan; George Gurdjieff's Institute for the Harmonious Development of Man in outer Paris; and Gerald Heard's Trabuco College in California. Throughout, Neima traces connections between the different communities, with founders and prominent members visiting and working with those covered elsewhere in the book. Common themes also emerge, such as commitment to internationalism and cooperation, rejection of materialism, the central role of arts and spirituality, willingness to experiment, and a lot of perseverance through hard work and disappointments.

The book will be valuable for those living in or seeking intentional community today who want to familiarize themselves with the shortcomings and successes of others who have gone before them. Readers more generally curious about this historical period will also find much here to speak to their imaginations.

—*Cameron Coombe, editor,*
EberhardArnold.com

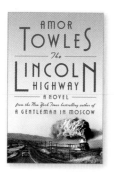

The Lincoln Highway
A Novel

Amor Towles
(Viking)

It's June 1954, and eight-year-old Billy lives with a neighbor in small-town Nebraska while his brother Emmett serves time in juvenile detention. At the start of Amor Towles's third novel, *The Lincoln Highway,* following *Rules of Civility* and *A Gentleman in Moscow,* Emmett is released early after the death of his father and escorted home by the warden.

Wishing to escape the town that remembers the fairground incident that landed him in detention for involuntary manslaughter, he and Billy decide to leave their father's failed farm and head for California in Emmett's only possession, a 1948 Studebaker Land Cruiser. But on the eve of their departure, Emmett is joined by Duchess and Woolly, two escaped delinquents from juvenile detention. Unbeknownst to Emmett, they had stowed themselves in the trunk of the warden's car. Emmett's plans for the future are no longer his own.

The misadventure continues when they all take to the road in the morning. Over the course of a ten-day road trip to California (sort of: they head east to New York) the boys encounter an improbable cast of heroes and villains. Towles artfully weaves critiques of racism, consumerism, affluence, and rootlessness into the text.

Although women's voices are scarce, two that appear offer some of the novel's keenest insights. Sally, the neighbor who cared for Billy, gets three pages of dialogue on the ordeal of making strawberry preserves, an old-fashioned chore that leaves her perspiring after a long, hot day in the kitchen. It is her metaphor for life: "Saying please and thank you is plenty old-fashioned. Getting married and raising children is old-fashioned. Traditions, the very means by which we come to know who we are, are nothing if not old-fashioned."

Toward the end of the book, Woolly's sister, Mrs. Whitney, another perceptive woman, muses that vice in too great a portion can hamper a life, but virtue can cause sorrow as well: "If you take a trait that by all appearances is a merit – a trait that is praised by pastors and poets, a trait that we have come to admire in our friends and hope to foster in our children – and you give it to some poor soul in abundance, it will almost certainly prove an obstacle to their happiness." Her sorrow for her bighearted, disaster-causing brother Woolly and her predicament with Dennis, her "too smart, too confident, or too hardworking" husband, weigh heavily.

There is poignancy in Mrs. Whitney's words: we all know people who, while not outright evil, take more than they should, let others clean up their mess, and sap the strength of those around them. But characters such as Sally, Mrs. Whitney, and the always honorable Emmett remind us that there are also plenty of people who give more than they take, forgive when they shouldn't, and carry those who fall. This reader's only disappointment was a too-abrupt ending.

—*Dori Moody,* Plough *managing editor*

> There are also plenty of people who give more than they take, forgive when they shouldn't, and carry those who fall.

PLOUGH BOOKLIST

New Release

Following the Call: Living the Sermon on the Mount Together

Eberhard Arnold, Augustine of Hippo, Wendell Berry, Dietrich Bonhoeffer, Dorothy Day, Meister Eckhart, Timothy Keller, Søren Kierkegaard, Martin Luther King Jr., C. S. Lewis, Richard Rohr, Dorothy L. Sayers, Rabindranath Tagore, Barbara Brown Taylor, Mother Teresa, Leo Tolstoy, N. T. Wright, and ninety-four others
Edited by Charles E. Moore

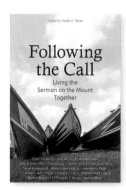

Jesus' most famous teaching, the Sermon on the Mount, possesses an irresistible quality. Who hasn't felt stirred and unsettled after reading these words, which get to the root of the human condition? This follow-up to the acclaimed collection *Called to Community* is designed to be read together with others, to engage and inspire communities of faith to discuss what it might look like to put these radical teachings into practice today.

Russell Moore, *Christianity Today*: As I read this collection, I tried to imagine the authors of the various reflections in conversation. What would Leo Tolstoy say to Karl Barth, or Francis of Assisi to Wendell Berry? The more I read, though, the more I started to imagine all of them in one place – listening to Jesus give the Sermon on the Mount. And, before long, I found myself blending into the crowd with them, hearing these strange, arresting, upending words of life. This book will prompt you to surprise, to delight, to melancholy, to argument, and, at every turn, will lead you back to Jesus.

See pages 115–119 for a sampling.

Softcover, 380 pages, ~~$18.00~~ **$10.80 with subscriber discount**

Companion volume:

Called to Community: The Life Jesus Wants for His People
Edited by Charles E. Moore
Foreword by Stanley Hauerwas

Why, in an age of connectivity, are our lives more isolated and fragmented than ever? And what can be done about it? Whether you have just begun thinking about communal living, are already embarking on sharing life with others, or have been part of a community for many years, the pieces in this collection will encourage, challenge, and strengthen you. The book's fifty-two chapters can be read one a week in group discussion.

Softcover, 378 pages, ~~$18.00~~ **$10.80 with subscriber discount**

Books That Cross Borders

From Red Earth: A Rwandan Story of Healing and Forgiveness

Denise Uwimana

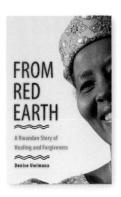

At the height of the Rwandan genocide, as men with bloody machetes ransacked her home, Denise Uwimana gave birth to her third son. With the unlikely help of Hutu Good Samaritans, she and her children survived. Her husband and other family members were not as lucky. Uwimana has devoted herself to the restoration of her country, empowering genocide widows to band together, tell their stories, find healing, and rebuild their lives.

Eric Irivuzumugabe, author, *My Father, Maker of the Trees*: Denise Uwimana speaks for our beautiful country, Rwanda, "land of a thousand hills." Her story details a people's struggle for healing and forgiveness in the wake of unimaginable horror. *From Red Earth* should be read by all people of faith to remind us that hope is stronger than hate.

Softcover, 232 pages, ~~$18.00~~ $10.80 with subscriber discount

Wisdom of the Sadhu: Teachings of Sundar Singh

Sadhu Sundar Singh

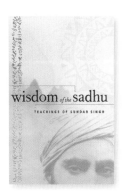

A modern Saint Francis, Sundar Singh (1889–1929) left his wealthy home in India at age sixteen to live as a wandering holy man. His beggar-like existence, his mystical encounters with Jesus, and his simple yet profound parables affected all who met him.

Robert Ellsberg, author, *All Saints*: Sadhu Sundar Singh is one of the most fascinating and enigmatic spiritual guides of the twentieth century. Rooted as it is in a distinctively Indian style, his Christian wisdom challenges Western readers to step beyond theological ideas and taste the gospel itself.

Softcover, 206 pages, ~~$15.00~~ $9.00 with subscriber discount

The 21: A Journey into the Land of Coptic Martyrs

Martin Mosebach

Foreword by Archbishop Angaelos

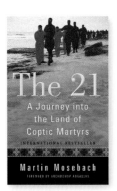

Behind a gruesome ISIS beheading video lies the untold story of the men in orange and the faith community that formed these unlikely modern-day saints and heroes. Writer Martin Mosebach traveled to the Egyptian village of El-Aour to meet the families of these young Coptic Christians, and better understand the faith and culture that shaped their convictions.

Cornerstone Forum: Mosebach asks us not to look away but rather to look directly into the faces and lives of these martyrs. By doing so, we of the lands of plenty and waning faith may find something that we have lost and may yet regain . . . but not without cost.

Softcover, 272 pages, ~~$18.00~~ $10.80 with subscriber discount

Christmas Gifts

Home for Christmas: Stories for Young and Old

Pearl Buck, Rebecca Caudill, Ruth Sawyer, Elizabeth Goudge, Selma Lagerlöf, Henry van Dyke, and others

They are some of the warmest childhood memories, those unhurried evenings around the fireplace, Christmas tree, or dinner table, when there was time for a story . . . Now, with this collection, you can keep the storytelling tradition alive in your family, and pass it on to your children or grandchildren.

    Home for Christmas includes twenty time-honored tales. Several are by world-famous authors; others are little-known treasures translated from other languages. Selected for their literary quality and spiritual integrity, they will resonate with readers of all ages, year after year. *Now in a deluxe hardcover gift edition.*

Jim Trelease, author, *The Read-Aloud Handbook*: If you're giving one book for Christmas, make it this one.

Hardcover, 339 pages, ~~$22.00~~ $13.20 with subscriber discount

Watch for the Light: Readings for Advent and Christmas

Dorothy Day, C. S. Lewis, Oscar Romero, Philip Yancey, Dietrich Bonhoeffer, Alfred Delp, Søren Kierkegaard, Annie Dillard, Kathleen Norris, and others

Though Christians the world over make yearly preparations for Lent, there's a conspicuous lack of good books for that other great spiritual season: Advent. Ecumenical in scope, these fifty devotions invite the reader to contemplate the great themes of Christmas and the significance that the coming of Jesus has for each of us – not only during Advent, but every day.

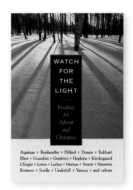

Publishers Weekly: These are not frivolous, feel-good Advent readings; they are deep, sometimes jarring reflections, many with a strong orientation toward social justice. . . . This collection, born of obvious passion and graced with superb writing, is a welcome – even necessary – addition to the glutted holiday bookshelves.

Hardcover, 344 pages, ~~$24.00~~ $14.40 with subscriber discount

Poems to See By: A Comic Artist Interprets Great Poetry

Julian Peters

This stunning anthology of favorite poems visually interpreted by comic artist Julian Peters breathes new life into some of the greatest English-language poets of the nineteenth and twentieth centuries. Poems are grouped in unexpected pairings around themes such as family, identity, creativity, time, mortality, and nature.

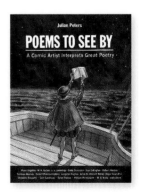

Wall Street Journal: Comics artist Julian Peters performs a sleight-of-paintbrush, as it were, with an array of powerful verses. . . . Mr. Peters writes that his motivation for translating great poetry into the visual language of comics was "for love of beauty." In this he has undoubtedly succeeded; reading *Poems to See By* is a stirring experience.

Hardcover, 160 pages, ~~$24.00~~ $14.40 with subscriber discount

Integrity *and the* Future of the Church

RUSSELL MOORE

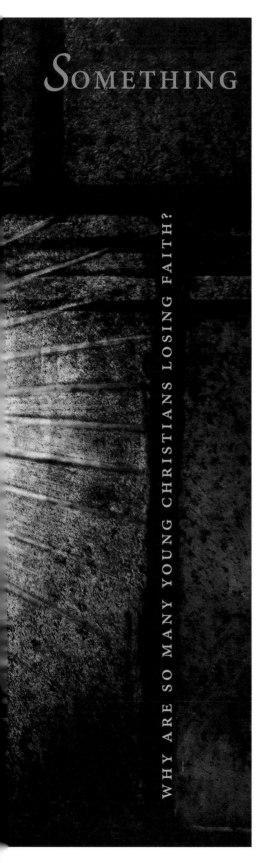

SOMETHING WAS HAPPENING AT THE VATICAN;

I cannot remember if the issue was another sexual abuse cover-up or a contentious synod meeting. But I do remember seeing a woman I knew to be a serious Roman Catholic post on her social media an old music video, with no commentary. The video, R.E.M.'s 1991 song "Losing My Religion," prompted friends to ask if she had lost her faith. She responded that she hadn't, but was afraid that she was losing her church. No wonder her friends were concerned. The song, after all, has entered popular culture as the soundtrack to almost any story of an ex-Catholic or an "ex-vangelical." To a haunting tune, the lyrics communicate both loss and confusion:

> That's me in the corner
> That's me in the spotlight
> Losing my religion
> Trying to keep up with you,
> And I don't know if I can do it
> Oh no, I've said too much
> I haven't said enough

R.E.M. lyrics were always cryptic, and, at least according to *American Songwriter* magazine, the lyrics to "Losing My Religion" are often misunderstood. The song is actually about anger – based on an old Southern expression: it's less "I don't find the ontological argument for theism believable anymore" and more "If I wait in this DMV line for one more minute, I'm fixing to lose my religion." In light of the current crisis of religion – seen perhaps most starkly in my own American evangelical subculture – I'm not sure that these are entirely different things. Perhaps "losing religion" now is about both interpretations of the song, if not as much about intellect and argumentation as about grief, betrayal, and anger.

When I was fifteen years old, I considered suicide – and it was because I didn't want to lose my religion. As I've written about elsewhere, I went through a prolonged spiritual crisis because of what I was seeing all around me in Bible Belt Christianity. Not only were there televangelist scandals all over the news, I knew that wasn't the half of it. Just as those in political journalism have long known how to interpret "Sen. Smith has decided to spend more time with his family," I knew how to interpret "the Lord has called Brother Jones from the pastorate into itinerant evangelism." I knew of "Christian people" who beat their children for listening to "secular music." I knew of "Christian people" who denounced vulgarity in the culture but seethed with racism. I heard prediction after prediction after prediction tying current events to Bible prophecy that was all "just about to happen." But nobody ever said, "Remember I told you Mikhail Gorbachev was probably the Antichrist? My bad," or, "Now that I also am using these supermarket scanners, maybe they're not the mark of the beast after all." These folks just moved on with their next confident assertions, as though the others had never happened at all.

And this was even more the case with politics. Even as a teenager, I could see that the voting guides that showed up in Bible Belt America were like the horoscopes in the newspaper – "today you will find a surprising new opportunity." A certain sort of credulous person is amazed at the accuracy without ever realizing that it's true for virtually everyone, virtually every day. Likewise, the voting guides divided the "Christian view" from the "anti-Christian view" on a list of issues that just happened to line up with the favored party's platform. Somehow, the Bible suddenly offered a "Christian view" on a balanced budget amendment or a line-item veto, things that had never been noticed until the favored candidates started emphasizing them. And along with all

that came apocalyptic warnings that if these candidates weren't elected, or those policies weren't enacted, we would "lose our entire culture." But when those candidates lost, no one headed for the bunkers. The culture didn't fall – at least not any more than it had before.

I started to wonder whether religion itself – or at least the kind of Christianity that showed up in the slogans all around me – might really be about something else: Southern culture or politics. If so, I thought, that would mean that Jesus is not the Way, the Truth, and the Life, but a means to an end. And that would mean that the gospel is not "you must be born again," but "you must be one of us." All that was terrifying to me because I really believed that Jesus was the Son of the living God. I really believed that Jesus loved me. And if the gospel I had been given was really just about finding ways to get voters to back party bosses or to fund prostitutes and cocaine for some preachers on TV, that would mean more than just an adolescent's cynical awakening. It would mean that the universe is a random, meaningless void; that the preacher who beat his daughter for dancing wasn't an aberration but was instead the way the cosmos is, right down to the core. And that was a horrible thought.

I had read *The Chronicles of Narnia* repeatedly as a child, so I recognized the name C. S. Lewis when I saw *Mere Christianity* in the bookstore – and the book re-oriented my life and my faith. What made the difference for me were not its arguments, but something much less describable, its tone and posture. I could tell that Lewis was not trying to sell me anything, to mobilize me, to prop up Bible Belt culture. His was not a means-to-an-end Christianity. And that was the wardrobe I needed to enter.

Russell Moore is public theologian at Christianity Today. *He is the author of six books, including* The Courage to Stand: Facing Your Fear Without Losing Your Soul *(B&H Books, 2020). Moore lives with his wife and five sons in Nashville, Tennessee.*

This would seem to be just a part of my personal story – or "testimony" as we would put it in my corner of Christianity – except that my fifteen-year-old self haunts me. I know that the reason I even went looking for C. S. Lewis is that I had been taught the Bible, in a good, loving church. I had seen genuine love and community and authenticity, week after week in Sunday school and Training Union and worship services and Vacation Bible Schools – I knew that it could exist, and what it would look like when I found it. But I wonder what would have happened to fifteen-year-old Russell Moore had I been born in 2001 instead of 1971. Would the things I saw have prompted a crisis at all? Or would I just have walked away altogether? Would I have ended up the sort of atheist or agnostic or "deconstructing ex-vangelical" that I find myself counseling almost every day now? I suppose I should just conclude that, with apologies to Paul Simon, I was born again at the right time.

My story, though, is hardly the only story. The number of Americans now affiliated with a church is just 47 percent. What's significant is not just the low number, but also the speed of the plummet – from 69 percent twenty years ago to 47 percent now. And the numbers are even worse than they appear. Generation X is less affiliated than Baby Boomers, Millennials less than Gen-X, and Generation Z looks likely to be even less affiliated than them all. In recent years, even some who were less apocalyptic about the prospects of evangelical Christianity – because of growth in the global South or the cyclical nature of revivals and awakenings – have grown more apprehensive about the prospects of evangelical Christianity in the twenty-first century. Referring to the "Nones," those claiming "no religious affiliation," Philip Jenkins contends that the future of the United States is None. Indeed, the most reliable studies available show us that as little as 8 percent of White Millennials identify as evangelicals, as compared to

26 percent of senior adults. With Generation Z, the numbers are even more jarring – with 34 percent (and growing) identifying as religiously unaffiliated.

What's more, the "culture wars" narrative of this secularization is increasingly demonstrated to be false – at least in the way it's been presented by and to American evangelicals over the past fifty years. Some disaffiliation, to be sure, is due to liberalizing cultural norms, decreasing fertility, and increasing mobility. But the evidence is mounting that a significant amount of secularization is accelerated and driven not by the "secular culture," but by evangelicalism itself. Many of us have observed, anecdotally, a hemorrhaging of younger evangelicals from churches and institutions in recent years. What seems different about this quiet exodus is that the departures are heightened not along the periphery of the church – among "nominal" or "cultural" Christians who grow up to rebel against their parents' beliefs – but among those who are *most* committed to what were previously thought to be the *hardest* aspects of Christian religion in modernity: belief in "the supernatural," accepting the rigorous demands of discipleship, longing for community and accountability in a multigenerational church with ancient roots and transcendent authority.

Where a "de-churched" (to use an anachronistic term) "ex-vangelical" (to use another) in the early 1920s was likely to have walked away because she found the virgin birth or the bodily resurrection outdated and superstitious or because he found moral libertinism more

MANY OF US HAVE OBSERVED A HEMORRHAGING OF YOUNGER EVANGELICALS FROM CHURCHES AND INSTITUTIONS IN RECENT YEARS.

attractive than the "outmoded" strict moral code of his past or because she wanted to escape the stifling bonds of a home church for an autonomous individualism, now we see a markedly different – and jarring – model of a disillusioned evangelical. We see young evangelicals walking away not because they do not believe what the church teaches, but because they believe the *church itself* does not believe what it teaches. This secularization comes

not from scientism and hedonism but disillusionment and cynicism. Many have pointed to compelling data showing that the politicization of American religion is a key driver-away from religious affiliation. Some would suggest that most of those leaving would identify politically as somewhere from moderate to progressive, to suggest that they are better off outside the church in the first place. Assuming, for the sake of argument, that's true, which comes first here? The demand to line up politically to follow Jesus or the decision to reject the politics of those making such demands? It seems to me that the problem is not actually specific political planks or ideas or personalities as much as it is that many have come to believe that the religion itself is a vehicle for the politics and cultural grievances, not the other way around.

WHAT HAPPENS WHEN PEOPLE REJECT THE CHURCH BECAUSE THEY THINK *WE* REJECT JESUS AND THE GOSPEL?

It's not difficult to see why. Twenty years ago I watched people suggesting that it was liberal Baptist theology that allowed many to wave away a president's sexual behavior as irrelevant to his office. Then I lived long enough to watch the same people suggest that those who *did not* wave away such behavior from another president might not be "real Christians." People can

change their minds, of course. But – as with the prophecy charts a generation ago – there is no talk of minds changing, just certainties in one direction and then certainties in the opposite. The only difference is the tribal affiliation of the leaders under discussion.

Trends toward secularization mean that people do not *need* the church in order to see themselves as Americans or as good people or even as "spiritual." And they certainly do not need the church in order to carry out their political affiliations – even when those political affiliations are those preferred by the church. If evangelicalism is politics, people can get their politics somewhere else – and fight and fornicate and get drunk too, if they want. A religion that calls people away from Western modernity will have to say, with credibility, "Take up your cross and follow me," not "Come with us, and we'll own the libs." You can do that on YouTube and not even give up a Sunday morning.

We might reassure ourselves, when we see the proliferating "Nones" among our youth, that the reason they are leaving is because they want to run their own lives and pursue the sexual hedonism the church (rightly) forbids. Some of that is no doubt the case. But if one believes the Bible one knows that wanting to run one's own life is not a modern development. And one need only know a little bit of high school biology to know that the desire for sexual hedonism didn't start in the Obama administration. First-century Athens, Greece, was just as intellectually averse to Christianity as twenty-first-century Athens, Georgia – and far more sexually "liberated" too. And the gospel went forth and the churches grew. The problem now is not that people think the church's way of life is too demanding, too morally rigorous, but that they have come to think the church doesn't believe its own moral teachings. The problem is not that they reject the idea that God could send anyone to hell but that, when they see the church covering up predatory behavior in its institutions, they have evidence that the church believes God would not send "our kind of people" to hell.

If people reject the church because they reject Jesus and the gospel, we should be saddened but not surprised. But what happens when people reject the church because they think *we* reject Jesus and the gospel? People have always left the church because they want to gratify the flesh, but what happens when people leave because they believe *the church* exists to gratify the flesh – in orgies of sex or anger or materialism? That's a far different problem. What if people don't leave the church because they disapprove of Jesus, but because they've read the Bible and have come to the conclusion that the church itself would disapprove of Jesus? That's a crisis.

Will the church die? No. The church moves out into the future not on the strength of its culture or its institutions but because of the promise of Jesus at Caesarea Philippi. And – however buffered the modern self might be from the so-called supernatural, the tomb is, in fact, empty. The apostles were telling the truth. The stories are true. And that means Jesus is alive – and seated in heaven until the kingdom of God has come on earth. That doesn't mean that the institutions as they are will continue to exist: any church can lose its lampstand, and any church "culture" can lose its credibility and die. The church will be reborn in every generation, but, as the prophet Jeremiah warned Jerusalem, "Don't be fooled by those who promise you safety simply because the Lord's temple is here. . . . Do you really think you can steal, murder, commit adultery, lie, and burn incense to Baal and all those other new gods of yours, and then come here and stand before me in my temple and chant, 'we are safe!' – only to go right back to all those evils again?" (Jer. 7:4, 8–10 NLT).

In 2 Kings 20, we find a strange incident with the king Hezekiah – an incident so

significant it is repeated almost verbatim later in Isaiah 39. Hezekiah – one of the few admirable kings described in the books of Kings and Chronicles – was healed of a disease, granted fifteen more years of life. His life, though, happened against the backdrop of the existential threat of Assyrian forces eager to conquer and overthrow. Envoys from Babylon traveled to Hezekiah's throne bearing from the Babylonian royal family letters and a gift, for they had heard of his sickness. "And Hezekiah welcomed them, and he showed them all his treasure house, the silver, the gold, the spices, the precious oil, his armory, all that was found in his storehouses," the Bible recounts. "There was nothing in his house or in all his realm that Hezekiah did not show them" (2 Kings 20:13). The prophet Isaiah approached the king, to ask what these envoys had seen. "And Hezekiah answered, 'They have seen all that is in my house; there is nothing in my storehouses that I did not show them'" (2 Kings 20:15). Isaiah's response was foreboding: he relayed an oracle from God that everything Hezekiah had stored up would one day be carted off to Babylon, and that some of Hezekiah's own sons would be exiles, eunuchs in the palace of the king of Babylon. God's denunciation is not (in this case) of the Babylonians. The problem is not that nations act as nations do, but Hezekiah. He had displayed before a potential geopolitical ally, and a potential geopolitical adversary, his power – his military might and economic wealth. At the moment, his values are their values. This is understandable; Hezekiah no doubt viewed the moment as a binary choice between the

Assyrians and the Babylonians.

Hezekiah, though, had seen a different sort of power in the past. He had, after all, been rescued from the valley of the shadow of death by God's mercy. When faced with the Assyrians' taunts of their might and power, Hezekiah took their letter and "went up to the house of the Lord and spread it before the Lord" (2 Kings 19:14). Hezekiah had seen how the bronze serpent – previously a sign of Israel's vulnerability (those dying from serpent venom looked to the image of the very thing plaguing them to be healed) – had been twisted into a totem of power, with the people of Israel making offerings to it (2 Kings 18:4). Just as Hezekiah's forefather David erred in seeking security in a census counting the people of God rather than the promise made to Abraham of a people more numerous than the sands of the shore or the stars of the sky, Hezekiah sought to counter verifiable strength with verifiable strength – as though Israel were just another nation, with just another transactional tribal god who would exchange protection for worship. What's instructive for American evangelicalism at the moment is not only Hezekiah's crisis of integrity, but also his response to the message of coming doom. "The word of the Lord that you have spoken is good," Hezekiah replied to Isaiah. "For he thought, 'Why not, if there will be peace and security in my days?'" (2 Kings 20:19).

In this, Hezekiah seemed to mistake the source of the kingdom's integrity. This was not about Hezekiah, but about a kingship that was rooted in a covenant with the House of David, to extend into the future as a house for God himself (2 Sam. 7). Hezekiah reassured himself about future judgment because of his present tranquility and safety. He was willing to sacrifice his children's future for his present moment.

This, of course, betrays the way of Moloch, not the way of the Son of David to come, who consecrated himself in order to stand before God with his brothers and sisters and say, "Behold, here am I and the children God has given to me" (Heb. 2:13). Hezekiah should have seen that fatherhood itself is about the future, is, as Christopher Hitchens once put it, a kind of "planned obsolescence" in which in our children we see the truth that they will face a future without us. To sacrifice the future for the sake of the present is a crisis of integrity, a crisis of faith.

Wendell Berry has suggested that some kinds of conservatism may be understood "in an adjectival sense," that one may be "cognizant of things worth conserving, and eager to conserve them, without being a conservative," in the sense of an ideological label. Evangelical Christians cannot be "conservative" without knowing what to conserve. This means knowing what to love. Only then will evangelical Christians see themselves as what they are meant to be: a renewal movement within the Body of Christ, charged with conserving for future generations the truth that "you must be born again," that the grace of God is personal and invitational, "just as I am, without one plea, but that thy blood was shed for me."

This real conservatism will look quite different from whatever slogans are bandied about by demagogues or mobs or even just by those who fear them or wish to remain in their good graces. When the next generation is told that the orthodox Christian belief in a God of both justice and justification is "Marxist," or that seeing morality as a matter of both personal and social responsibility is "critical race theory," they can tell that even the labelers do not believe what they're saying. When the next generation sees sexual abuse covered up – and those who call it out silenced or shamed – they see a use of power quite different from that of a Good Shepherd. When they see evangelicalism as a political interest group, they can easily see where the ground of unity actually is. And what they are really asking is about integrity – about whether all of this holds together. What they ask is not "Can I believe what you are saying?" but "Do you believe what you are saying?" The challenge for evangelical Christianity is whether we will say, with the Apostle Paul: "To them we did not yield in submission even for a moment, so that the truth of the gospel might be preserved for you" (Gal. 2:5 ESV). Challenging an evangelical movement about conduct that is "not in step with the truth of the gospel" (Gal. 2:14 ESV) often prompts a charge of fostering disunity – along with warnings about how important it is to remain unified in such trying times. Yet unity is not silence before injustice, or the hoarding of temporal influence, but a concern for the one, holy, catholic, and apostolic church, which includes those who came before and those who come after – provided that the scandal they encounter is the scandal of the cross rather than the scandal of us.

Contemplating my warning, some will no doubt ask, "But where is the hope?" In this case, the diagnosis is the cure. What we are called to do is to repent – to turn around. As the prophet Jeremiah wrote: "Set up road markers for yourself; make yourself guideposts; consider well the highway, the road by which you went" (Jer. 31:21 ESV). A drowning Simon Peter did not need a nautical map or the foreknowledge of nuclear submarine technology. He needed to cry out "Lord, save me," and to grab hold of the hand that could pull him up again (Matt. 14:30-31).

Meanwhile, we must rebuild our integrity without yielding to cynicism. Our institutions have sometimes failed us; Jesus has not. If the church is the temple of the living God, made up of living stones, we must remember how Jesus responds to temples. Faced with a temple compromised both vertically ("a house

of prayer") and horizontally ("for all people"), Jesus overturned the status quo, and spoke of building the temple anew, a claim so shocking it was repeated as one of the charges of blasphemy and political disloyalty he would face on the way to the Place of the Skull. When he overturned tables, the people thought Jesus was violating God's temple when in fact it was his zeal for the temple that led to anger at what it had become. They thought he was "losing his religion" in the theological sense, but he was losing his religion in the Southern folk-language sense. He can do so again – perhaps he is even now.

OUR INSTITUTIONS HAVE SOMETIMES FAILED US; JESUS HAS NOT.

The church will survive – even here in America – but, along the way, a lot of fifteen-year-olds will be hurt. A lot of them will conclude that the gospel is just one more aspect of political theater or outrage culture or institutional self-perpetuation or worse. They will be wrong, of course, but, as Jesus put it, "woe to the one by whom the stumbling block comes" (Matt. 18:7). We are losing too many of a generation – not because they are secularists, but because they believe we are. What this demands is not rebranding, but repentance – a turnaround. Stranger things have happened, and that's good, because we will need stranger things. We need to be the people of Christ and him crucified, the people of a Word that stands above all earthly powers and, no thanks to them, abides. Somewhere out there, there's at least one fifteen-year-old losing his religion who needs to see if we're such a people.

Maybe, even, his life depends on it. ⟿

This talk was given at the Plough Writers Weekend on August 7, 2021, at the Fox Hill Bruderhof in New York.

ANN THOMAS

How to Run a Cemetery

A graveyard is a place where people laugh, feud, suffer – and where they can find a grace that crosses the border between worlds.

"THESE TWO? These are the ones we want!" The woman, with a twirl of her wrists and a sweeping motion of her slender arms, approximated through her gesture the area she and her husband had settled on. It was a flourish more fitting for a game show than two graves. He nodded to his wife in confirmation, participating via cell phone from their son's car on the cemetery's driveway, where he sat, too weak to get out. The labor exerted in his simple nod was a sobering contrast to the vivacity of his wife, also in her seventies.

Gathered around their daughter's cell phone, we documented their arrangements, under the shade of the thick timber that creeps yearly closer to our platted graves. The sparse grass growing in filtered sun where we stood was a fair trade for goldfinches and orioles nesting nearby, and bluebirds enticed to take up residence in little boxes on the ravine's perimeter. It was too perfect a spring day to lose minutes doing the paperwork in an office. We were almost finished, when they had one more question.

"Shall we see if we fit?"

"'Try before you buy' is a great policy, though I don't get many takers on it here," I pretended to muse. "But sure. Why not?" This family was *playful*, taking the task at hand seriously, but not resisting the joy we all found in such a beautiful afternoon. I couldn't help being drawn into their dynamic.

Her husband nodded again from the car, this time towards their daughter. "Seriously? Okay." She ended the call with her father, pulled up her camera app, and handed me her phone. "Where," she asked me, "where exactly are my parents going to be?"

"Bride on the left and groom on the right, just like at their wedding. Facing east to rise and greet the Last Day." I extended my left foot and tapped the middle of her mother's grave; then, pacing south through the increment of measure in my legs' muscle memory, I tapped the center of his grave. "Your father will be right here."

She lay down alongside her teenage son, who had quietly wandered through neighboring headstones until called upon to proxy for his grandmother, and I took pictures as they asked. Her father smiled at us from the passenger window as he watched me help his daughter stand up and brush off the blades of his grave's grass that clung to her hair and blouse.

No one prepared me for moments like this, or anything else, when I became sexton of our Catholic cemetery. I was simply given a standard receipt book you can purchase at any office supply store, and an array of maps and records of the cemetery's 125 years. There were leather-bound folios written with fountain pen in elegant cursive, and small notebooks logging the penciled scrawlings of barely literate, grave-digging drunkards, up through our current spreadsheets. The rest was left for me to discover.

Several matters required collaboration from a number of professionals: funeral directors, gravediggers, monument-company employees, and the elusive engraver. He darted in and out of cemeteries all over the state, adding death dates to headstones of recent burials where either tall heaps of dirt waited to be settled by rains, or wreaths over discreet openings marked cremations. Often I'd learn of his presence on the grounds only by his air compressor's distant drone, and before I had a chance to say hello I'd hear his pickup rattling out of our cemetery and on to the next.

Other matters we managed individually, and for me, this meant appointments to purchase graves. Many would begin with an apology: "I'm sorry, I don't know how to buy a grave. I don't know where to start." This was the easiest beginning, and one I always hoped for.

"I'm so relieved to hear that," I'd say, and mean it. "It would be terrible if you'd had enough practice to become good at it. You don't need to apologize. I'll walk you through everything, literally." I'd start with the outline of what they needed to consider: Do you already have family here you want to be near? Do you

Katherine Tucker,
*Old Times There
Are Not Forgotten*,
oil on panel, 2015

Ann Thomas is a writer and poet whose work has appeared in Image, Forma, *and* St. Austin Review. *She is the managing editor of* Dappled Things, *and lives with her husband and five children in Iowa City, Iowa.*

want an upright monument or a flat headstone? How many family members are you hoping to be buried alongside? Have you thought about if you will be cremated or have a traditional full burial? Always the same questions, always the same order.

We'd talk through their thoughts as we walked through the graves.

THE CIRCUMSTANCES of our walks never dictated how difficult a family might be to help. In fact, often the most difficult to assist were those who were not in need of a grave anytime soon, or who had lost loved ones long ago. Among them were a number who demanded to know exactly who I've lost and how I grieve them, or perhaps wished death upon my husband and children so I would be overwhelmed by my own suffering. There were those who for decades would refuse to let grass grow on their loved one's grave, even fighting with family to the point of obtaining a permit to exhume remains and not telling anyone where they were taken.

To my wonder, families with the most tragic circumstances were among my most grace-filled encounters, those who found themselves walking with me unexpectedly. Parents lost children, wives and husbands were struck with the unforeseen death of a young spouse, immigrants dealt with the realization that longed-for reunions won't happen this side of life, illness progressed more rapidly than anticipated.

Many regard a cemetery as a thin place, a liminal space where the veil between us and eternity is almost transparent. But while the ground is consecrated, set aside for a sacred purpose, it is not the physical location itself that precipitates such grace. It is of no consequence how narrow a margin lies between life and death. Only God's love creates communion through space and time. That was the only thing that could be sustaining some of these families, and it was utterly humbling to witness.

How do I know it is God's love, not just a matter of being swept along by emotions? Were, maybe, these families just lucky that something worse had never happened to them, they weren't sicker, or poorer, or had more nasty breaks to push them over the edge? No; I know their stories and I know these things did happen to them, and more besides.

I know it is God's love because I was humbled before it the same way I'm humbled in receiving the Eucharist, the Sacrament of Love, knowing I am unworthy, one of the workers called late in the day and given a full wage (Matt. 20:1–16). The full wage was a participation in another family's love, the fruit of their patient bearing of struggles with each other and the world, their suffering, and especially with discerning and accepting God's will for themselves and their families. Although at some level all who sought rest for their loved ones in a Catholic cemetery shared the same faith, these families bore it out in a different way.

The secret I learned from these grace-filled witnesses is that while there is no escaping death, they have found ways to die before they are dead: to themselves in sacrifice for others, to the world in their refusal to chase gains that they cannot store up for the next life. Most of all, they hope. They live the death they are baptized into in Christ, and in hope they are saved from despair in their suffering; the end of their own or their loved one's life on earth really is a matter of being born to eternal life. As they begin that new life, we rejoice amid the sorrow. Joy and sorrow do not cancel each other out. There can be both in each death.

> For in hope we were saved. Now hope that sees for itself is not hope. For who hopes for what one sees? But if we hope for what we do not see, we wait with endurance. (Rom. 8:24–25)

We speak about "having hope" as if it were a substance one could possess, but after working in the cemetery, I think of it as space, a field to be cultivated. That field holds the treasure of eternal life; it's the same one the merchant sells all he owns to purchase (Matt. 13:44). That field grants us the ability to accommodate all we encounter: the sorrow, the doubt, the suffering, the pain we inevitably face no matter who we are, where we live. It explains the inexpressible vastness I experienced with these families that made space for everyone and everything in their lives and kept them from being crushed under the weight of it. These families were sustained in the valley of the shadow of death, purchasing a fullness of life, a treasure buried in that field of hope, which we come into possession of through dying to ourselves now and ultimately at the hour of earthly death.

Any liminality I experienced with a family was because of their own intimacy with God, their own desire to make God present in ordinary moments each day, their own patient endurance, and the expansion of their field

to include me in their love. They cleared and cultivated space for each other and the divine throughout their lives, and their striving came

---

We speak about "having hope" as if it were a substance one could possess, but after working in the cemetery, I think of it as space, a field to be cultivated.

---

to full blossom before I walked with them as they prepared to bury someone they loved. I just enjoyed the fragrance.

OUR FAMILY'S CIRCUMSTANCES changed, and I needed to resign from the cemetery. My last afternoon there was spent waiting for an appointment with someone who never showed. As I began my final walk through the graves alone to my car, I heard the engraver's truck rattle to a stop in front of the chapel.

"John! You showed up for my last day! How thoughtful of you," I teased as he opened his trailer to pull out his gear.

"Ann! Quitting? Had enough?"

These families were sustained in the valley of the shadow of death, purchasing a fullness of life, a treasure buried in that field of hope.

"Of some of it, yes. That's not why though. I'm glad I get to say goodbye, but I won't keep you, I know you've got somewhere to rush off to."

"No! Last stone of the *season!* No hurry today." This was the final late-fall day that the stones would hold enough warmth to be engraved; with the onset of cold, the attempt to sandblast might crack them. The last name on John's list was our lovely "Fearless Frieda," a frequent visitor to the cemetery, who had died a few weeks earlier at 103. The headstone she shared with her husband, black granite and

flush with the ground, had marked his grave for decades, in the very southwesternmost corner of our cemetery. She had a gray bench placed in front of it to rest on during her visits, but now they were side by side again: bride on the left, groom on the right. Her secret to a long life, we'd deduced, must have had something to do with the St. Pauli Girl Lager she kept on hand for guests, and partook of through her late nineties.

John and I leaned against his truck, talking for a long time about a lot of things, but mostly cemeteries.

"You gonna be buried here?" he asked.

"No, I want to be buried northeast of here. About three hours away, along the Mississippi."

"That's where you're from?"

"Sort of. I want to be far away so no one ever visits my grave. I don't want a stone, don't care if my grave's marked, don't care if anyone can find me once I'm dead." Knowing how I love the ravine at the heart of the cemetery, how I spend time with my children there hiking especially in fall when deer are easy to spot through naked timber, this initially surprised him. After some thought, he understood.

For all the cemeteries he has worked in, John has experienced more than anyone how the living can be swallowed up by graves. "Every night, around supper, that's when cemeteries get busy. You wouldn't believe how many cemeteries have the same folks visit their husbands or wives every night, their children." I knew of our regulars, who came every day. I didn't want to think how widespread a phenomenon it truly is, but John knows. Their hope seems buried with their loved ones, only ever cultivating the same four-by-eleven-feet dimensions of the grave.

"Your husband okay with that?"

"Of course he's not!" We both laughed. "It probably won't happen, but that's what I want." ⇴

Daring to Follow the Call

The Sermon on the Mount in Daily Life

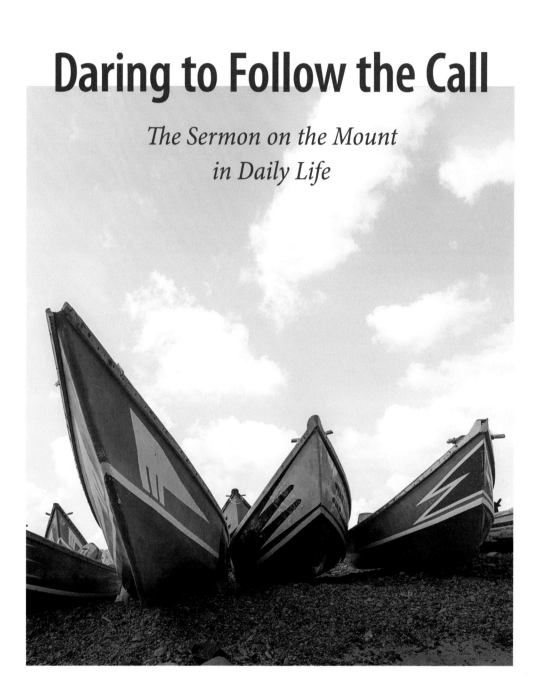

Image by John M Lund Photography Inc/Getty Images. Used by permission.

Readings from E. Stanley Jones, Barbara Brown Taylor, Teresa of Ávila, Oscar Romero, Martin Luther King Jr., Eberhard Arnold, Meister Eckhart, Leonardo Boff, C. S. Lewis, Hermas, and Dietrich Bonhoeffer

Following the Call: Living the Sermon on the Mount Together, a new *Plough* anthology of weekly readings, brings together insights on the Sermon on the Mount from a wealth of traditions (see page 99). From the book:

Beyond Duty

E. Stanley Jones

There is a "beyondness" in the Sermon on the Mount that startles and appalls the legalistic mind. It sees no limit to duty – the first mile does not suffice, he will go two; the coat is not enough, he will give the cloak also; to love friends is not enough, he will love enemies as well. Come to that with the legalistic mind and it is impossible and absurd; come to it with the mind of the lover and nothing else is possible. The lover's attitude is not one of duty, but one of privilege. Here is the key to the Sermon on the Mount. We mistake it entirely if we look on it as the chart of the Christian's duty; rather, it is the charter of the Christian's liberty – his liberty to go beyond, to do the thing that love impels and not merely the thing that duty compels.

Quino Al / unsplash

Exceeding Righteousness

Barbara Brown Taylor

I am so sorry to tell you this, but Jesus was just not a very good Protestant. He was a Jew, for whom good works were not optional. He was the loving son of the Light-Giver who gave the law, and he expected those who followed him to follow it too, right down to the last jot and tittle. Later Paul would mount some good arguments about how the law was God's grace for Jews, while God had something different in mind for Gentiles. But however our view of the law has changed through the years, our spiritual ancestors had the good sense to preserve this core teaching of Jesus in the Sermon on the Mount: God expects us to step up. Righteousness is a good thing. Exceeding righteousness is even better. Knowing God's word is no substitute for doing it.

E. Stanley Jones, *A Working Philosophy of Life* (Potomac, MD: E. Stanley Jones Foundation, 2017), 36–37. Barbara Brown Taylor, "The Grace of Good Works," sermon preached in Duke University Chapel, February 9, 2014.

The Meek
Teresa of Ávila

Who can say that he possesses any virtue, or that he is rich, if at the time when he most needs this virtue he finds himself devoid of it? No, let us rather think of ourselves as lacking it and not run into debt without having the means of repayment. Our treasure must come from elsewhere and we never know when God will leave us in this prison of our misery without giving us any. If others, thinking we are good, bestow favors and honors upon us, both they and we shall look foolish when, as I say, it becomes clear that our virtues are only lent us. The truth is that, if we serve the Lord with humility, he will sooner or later succor us in our needs. But, if we are not strong in this virtue, the Lord will leave us to ourselves, as they say, at every step. This is a great favor on his part, for it helps us to realize fully that we have nothing which has not been given us.

Persecuted Because of Righteousness
Oscar Romero

This is the mission entrusted to the church, a difficult mission: to uproot sins from history, to uproot sins from politics, to uproot sins from the economy, to uproot sins from wherever they are. What a difficult task! The church has to confront conflicts caused by great selfishness, great pride, and great vanity because so many people have enthroned the kingdom of sin among us. The church must suffer for speaking the truth, for denouncing sin, and for uprooting sin. No one wants to have a sore spot touched, and therefore a society with so many sores reacts strongly when someone has the

courage to touch the sore and say: "You have to treat that. You have to eliminate that. Believe in Christ and be converted."

Turn the Other Cheek
Martin Luther King Jr.

Through violence you may murder the liar, but you cannot murder the lie, nor establish the truth. Through violence you may murder the hater, but you do not murder hate. In fact, violence merely increases hate. So it goes. Returning violence for violence multiplies violence, adding deeper darkness to a night already devoid of stars. Darkness cannot drive out darkness; only light can do that. Hate cannot drive out hate; only love can do that.

Saint Teresa of Ávila, *The Way of Perfection*, translated by E. Allison Peers (New York: Image Books, 1964), 148–149. Oscar Romero, *A Prophetic Bishop Speaks to His People: The Complete Homilies of Archbishop Oscar Arnulfo Romero*, vol. 2, trans. Joseph Owens, SJ (Miami: Convivium Press, 2015), 203. Martin Luther King Jr., "Where Do We Go from Here?" speech, Eleventh Annual SCLC Convention, Atlanta, Georgia, August 16, 1967.

Bakr Magrabi / Pexels

Thy Kingdom Come

Eberhard Arnold

Prayer must never supplant work. If we sincerely ask God for his will to be done, for his nature to be revealed in our work, for his rule to bring humankind to unity, justice, and love, then our life will be one of work. Faith without works is dead. Prayer without work is hypocrisy. Unless we actively work to build for God's kingdom, the Lord's Prayer – "Your kingdom come" – is a lie on our lips. The purpose of Jesus' prayer is to bring us to the point where its meaning is lived out, where it actually happens and becomes part of history. Each of us needs to find a way to devote our whole working strength so that God is honored, his will is done, and his kingdom comes.

Thy Will Be Done

Meister Eckhart

We deafen God day and night with our words, "Lord, thy will be done." But then when God's will does happen, we are furious and don't like it a bit. When our will becomes God's will, that is certainly good; but how much better it would be if God's will were to become our will. But as it is now, when you are sick, of course you don't want to be well against God's will, but you wish that it were God's will for you to get well. . . . Anyone who by God's grace unites his will purely and completely with God's will has no need other than to say in his ardent longing: "Lord, show me what is thy dearest will and give me strength to do it!" And God will do this, as truly as he lives, and to such a one he will give in great abundance and all perfection.

Our Daily Bread

Leonardo Boff

The need for bread is an individual matter, but the satisfaction of that need cannot be an individual effort; it must be that of a community. Thus we do not pray "my Father," but "our Father." . . . This bread that is jointly produced must be distributed and consumed in concert with others. Only then can we truthfully ask for *our* daily bread. God does not hear the prayer that asks only for *my* bread. A genuine relationship with God calls for maintaining a relationship with others. When we present God with our own needs, he wants us to include those of our brothers and sisters. Otherwise the bonds of fellowship are severed and we live only for ourselves. We all share the same basic necessity; collective satisfaction of that need makes us brothers and sisters.

Africa Studio / Shutterstock

Eberhard Arnold, *The Prayer God Answers* (Walden, NY: Plough Publishing House, 2016), 37. Meister Eckhart, *Meister Eckhart spricht* (Munich: Verlag Ars Sacra/Josef Müller Verlag, 1925), selections translated by *Plough* editors. Leonardo Boff, *Praying with Jesus and Mary* (Maryknoll, NY: Orbis Books, 2005), 78–79.

Two Ways

C. S. Lewis

The more you obey your conscience, the more your conscience will demand of you. And your natural self, which is thus being starved and hampered and worried at every turn, will get angrier and angrier. In the end, you will either give up trying to be good, or else become one of those people who, as they say, "live for others" but always in a discontented, grumbling way – always wondering why the others do not notice it more and always making a martyr of yourself. And once you become that you will be a far greater pest to anyone who has to live with you than you would have been if you had remained frankly selfish.

The Christian way is different: harder, and easier. Christ says, "Give me All. I don't want so much of your time and so much of your money and so much of your work: I want You. I have not come to torment your natural self, but to kill it. No half-measures are any good. I don't want to cut off a branch here and a branch there, I want to have the whole tree down. I don't want to drill the tooth, or crown it, or stop it, but to have it out. Hand over the whole natural self, all the desires which you think innocent as well as the ones you think wicked – the whole outfit. I will give you a new self instead. In fact, I will give you myself: my own will shall become yours."

Put the Lord in Your Heart

Hermas

"Sir, these commandments are great and good and glorious, and are able to gladden the heart of the one who is able to keep them. But I do not know if these commandments can be kept by a human, for they are very hard.". . . "Those who have the Lord in their heart,"

he said, "can master everything, including all these commandments. But to those who have the Lord on their lips but whose heart is hardened and who are far from the Lord, these commandments are hard and difficult. You, therefore, who are empty and fickle in the faith, put the Lord in your heart and you will realize that nothing is easier or sweeter or more gentle than these commandments."

Whoever Hears These Words

Dietrich Bonhoeffer

Humanly speaking, we could understand and interpret the Sermon on the Mount in a thousand different ways. Jesus knows only one possibility: simple surrender and obedience, not interpreting it or applying it, but doing and obeying it. . . . He does not mean that it is to be discussed as an ideal, he really means us to get on with it. ⤳

The Shepherd of Hermas, *The Apostolic Fathers,* third edition, ed. and trans. Michael W. Holmes (Grand Rapids, MI: Baker Academic, 2007), 549–551. C. S. Lewis, *Mere Christianity* (New York: HarperOne: 2001), 196–197. Dietrich Bonhoeffer, *The Cost of Discipleship*, trans. Reginald H. Fuller (London: SCM Press, 1959), 175.

Toyohiko Kagawa

Pacifist Patriot, Christian Socialist, Incendiary Peacemaker

SUSANNAH BLACK *and* **JASON LANDSEL**

ON CHRISTMAS EVE, 1909, Toyohiko Kagawa, a twenty-one-year-old seminarian, moved into the Shinkawa slum district of Kobe, Japan, to share a home with down-and-outs, feeding them from his student stipend.

The illegitimate son of a samurai, Kagawa had been orphaned at age four. At school, he was welcomed into the households of American Presbyterian missionaries. Their love, and love of learning, was infectious. "For the first time," Kagawa recalled, "I began to awaken to a sense of being alive." He read Ruskin, Tolstoy, and the Bible.

Kagawa became convinced that he had to care for the poor personally. But after moving into the slum, he realized that this would not be enough. How could he help demoralized people *want* to take care of themselves? How could the economy be changed so people would have a chance to thrive? What could he do to keep families together so children would not grow up without love?

Kagawa found a wife, Haru Shiba, who shared wholeheartedly in his ministry. When their first baby came along in 1922, they moved out of the slum, where infant mortality was 75 percent. But Kagawa continued tirelessly organizing and writing. Inspired by English guild socialism, he focused on building worker cooperatives and labor unions. And he became active in the international peace movement, speaking out against militarism and imperialism.

Still, Kagawa considered himself a patriot.

After Japan bombed Pearl Harbor and the United States entered World War II, he made radio broadcasts condemning American barbarism while failing to similarly condemn Japanese atrocities. Even so, his record of pacifism, such as his public apology to China for Japan's invasion of Manchuria, made him suspect, and he was arrested twice for "antiwar thoughts."

With the US nuclear bombing of Hiroshima and Nagasaki, the war was over. In February 1946, a much-diminished Emperor Hirohito, no longer officially considered divine, called Kagawa to the Imperial Palace. "Whoever wishes to be great among you must become the servant of all," Kagawa advised, quoting Jesus. "A ruler's sovereignty, Your Majesty, is in the hearts of his people. Only by service to others can a man, or nation, be godlike."

As an adviser in the postwar reconstruction, Kagawa saw many of the reforms he had sought realized – legalized unions, redistribution of land, worker cooperatives, and women's suffrage. It took losing the war that had compromised his mission for that mission to be fulfilled.

Kagawa wrote more than one hundred fifty books, including bestselling novels. He was twice nominated for the Nobel Prize in Literature, four times for the Nobel Peace Prize. A pacifist patriot, a socialist Christian, and an incendiary peacemaker, he wasn't always the saint he was made out to be. But he never lost the conviction that because God cares for each person, so must we. ➤

Susannah Black is a Plough *editor.* *Jason Landsel is the artist for* Plough's *"Forerunners" series.*